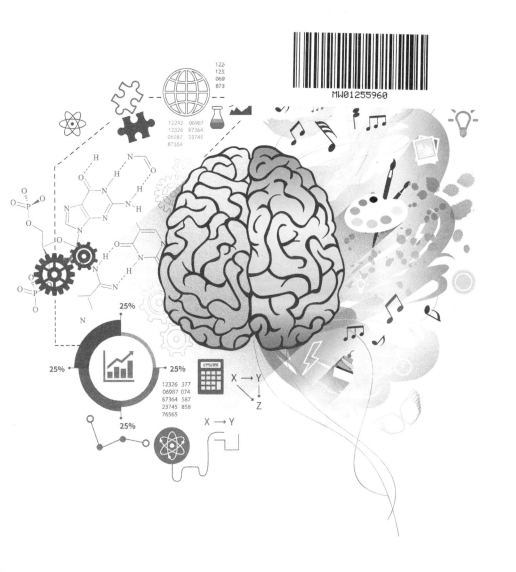

DEMYSTIFYING
Learning Styles
WHAT EVERY HOMESCHOOL PARENT NEEDS TO KNOW

TYLER H. HOGAN

DEMYSTIFYING LEARNING STYLES

by

Tyler H. Hogan

Demystifying Learning Styles

What Every Homeschool Parent Needs to Know

by Tyler H. Hogan

© 2018 Bright Ideas Press

ISBN: 978-1-892427-64-9 (Print)

ISBN: 978-1-892427-63-2 (Digital)

Bright Ideas Press
Dover, Delaware
Vero Beach, Florida

www.BrightIdeasPress.com

877.492.8081

24 23 22 21 20 19 18   7 6 5 4 3 2 1

Layout and design by Tyler H. Hogan & Melissa E. Craig

For Helen,
who never ceases to inspire me

If to do were as easy as to know what were good to do,

chapels had been churches, and poor men's cottages princes'

palaces. It is a good divine that follows his own instructions; I

can easier teach twenty what were good to be done than to be one

of the twenty to follow mine own teaching.

      —Portia, *The Merchant of Venice*, Act I, Scene 2

CONTENTS

INTRODUCTION

Helping our children learn can be challenging. Often, the methods that worked for us in school don't seem to work for our kids. A lesson we review ad nauseam is forgotten the next day, and we're met with a blank expression or "I don't remember ever talking about that." It can feel like we and our kids are speaking different languages while we teach.

Parents and teachers through the ages have attempted to discover the magic key to unlock our students' learning. Theories and philosophies of education abound. Cognitive science, neuroscience, and psychology each try to shed light on how the brain and the mind work. Our own experiences as students with exceptional, mediocre, and infamous teachers color our approach and practice. Trying to sort through the countless books and papers on learning styles and pedagogical methods is daunting and may leave a parent or teacher feeling more confused than ever. Some theories make perfect sense intuitively but lack scientific study to bear them out.

Taking a scientific approach to this topic is challenging for several reasons. First, the literature on learning styles is voluminous and contradictory. Hundreds of models of learning styles, with a great deal of overlap, have been proposed over the last 150 years. The ones that have risen to the top of the stack have very little to do with one another, making synthesis difficult. Further, for each study published on the topic, we can find another paper or study debunking or contradicting its conclusions. Second, there seems to be a divide between the studies on education and the studies on psychology, cognitive science, and neuroscience. For some reason, the education world and the scientific community don't seem to be sharing notes, which is a real shame. Finally, the nature of studies in these areas is inherently complicated. Social sciences (including education and psychology) don't have the same kind of reproducibility and firmness of conclusions that we expect from hard sciences like physics and chemistry. A foundational study on learning theories performed in 1955 (which hundreds of further papers cite) may be suddenly thrown into question when attempts to reproduce the original study today yield a different result. We can't state "Student + Instructional Model A = Learning" with the same certainty as "2 + 2 = 4."

In this (mercifully short) book, I aim to summarize what I have learned in my years of research and experience as a student, parent, teacher, and curriculum developer. We will go over some of the most influential theories of learning, such as the multistore model of memory, Drs. Rita and Kenneth Dunn's work on environmental preferences, the VAK modalities, Dr. Howard Gardner's theory of multiple intelligences, with helpful additions from other prominent theories and researchers. We will discuss how students take in and recall information, how to help them pay attention and concentrate, how to motivate them, and how to plan and assess their learning. We will study the ways in which all of us learn, and we'll discuss learning factors that vary from student to student. We'll explore strategies for how to leverage your own strengths and your students' strengths, and we'll discuss strategies for making learning engaging for everyone in your home or classroom. My hope is that this will be a great help for new and experienced educators alike, whether you teach your own kids at home or work in a classroom setting.

CHAPTER 1

THE POWER OF

MEMORY

HOW MEMORY WORKS

We can take it as axiomatic that memory is foundational to learning. If a skill or a piece of information is not readily accessible from long-term memory, can it really be said that someone has learned it? One of our goals as educators is to help our students remember that which is important. Certainly, we expect that much of what we say may be forgotten, and we have to make a certain amount of peace with that. However, the things that are most important—the things that absolutely must enter students' long-term memory—are the things that require the most effective strategies for ensuring recall.

Fortunately, cognitive science provides a great deal of insight into how memories are formed. Cognitive science studies the mind—our thoughts, memories, and decision-making processes. It melds the hard science of neurology with the soft science of psychology, using both brain scans and behavioral experiments to form the basis of its theories and models. While no science is ever perfect, cognitive science has many illuminating ideas that are extremely useful to every parent and teacher.

> *One of our goals as educators is to help our students remember that which is important.*

Much of the literature on learning styles is focused on each student's individuality and unique stylistic make-up. The challenge in applying those principles lies in identifying a particular student's needs and matching our instructional strategy to that student. However, when it comes to memory, we don't need to take quite as individualized an approach. The manner in which information moves from our senses to our long-term memory is fairly consistent from person to person. (There are exceptions to this when dealing with learning disabilities, brain damage, diseases such as Alzheimer's disease, and other unusual cases; however, these situations are beyond the scope of this book.)

Our Three Memory Banks

Cognitive scientists present a multistore model of memory. It starts with recognizing that we have three banks of memory: sensory memory, working memory, and long-term memory.

Sensory memory is where we take in all of the stimuli that our bodies constantly notice through all of our senses. As you read this, you're receiving a great deal of sensory input. You can feel your tongue inside your mouth. You may hear the whir of the HVAC system, the noise of children, people talking, traffic, or birds in the background. Your heat receptors are letting you know if your body is too hot or too cold. You can feel if any of your muscles are tight or if your feet hurt from standing too long. Everything you see—whether it's something in your peripheral vision or the words that you are looking at on this page—is flooding into your sensory memory.

You're taking in a tremendous amount of information. In fact, it's more than any brain can process simultaneously. But that's okay because, frankly, most of your sensory input is not relevant to your current goals. The fact that you can feel your tongue inside of your mouth does not mean that you need to focus on it. Our brains do a pretty remarkable job of filtering out extraneous sensory information. That filter is what we call attention. When you pay attention, what you are doing is setting your filter so that it allows a certain subset of your sensory input to make its way into the next memory bank: the working memory.

We can focus our attention volitionally. However, in the absence of an act of will, the brain will default to paying attention to whatever it regards as most important. (And that's generally not what teachers consider important.) This is why it can feel so difficult to pay attention when we're hungry, tired, stressed, or ill. The brain might deem our hunger, need for sleep, a fight-or-flight response to stress, or a painful splinter as more important than, say, a lecture on George Washington. And there is very little we can do about that, aside from either meeting those bodily needs first or exerting Herculean levels of willpower.

> *We can focus our attention volitionally. However, in the absence of an act of will, the brain will default to paying attention to whatever it regards as most important. (And that's generally not what teachers consider important.)*

The sensory input that makes it through our attention filter goes into our working memory. Working memory is very similar to RAM on a computer. It's the short list of things that we are currently and actively thinking about or holding in our minds. We all know this intuitively, but it is very important to understand that working memory is limited. There are many ideas about exactly how limited our working memory is, but no one really knows for sure. It is safe to say that the amount of space for working memory varies from person to person. Some scientists postulate that the number of items (or sets of items) is between five and nine. We won't go into all of the debate surrounding that number, but it is much lower than many of us imagined, and it has significant implications for our teaching practices. The amount of working memory that is in use at any given moment is called cognitive load. We will discuss cognitive load in more detail in chapter 2.

Our third memory bank is long-term memory. This is the final destination for any piece of information worth recalling later on; at least that's the goal. We might think of our long-term memory as a filing cabinet complete with a robust index. The skills and bits of information are filed away in the cabinet, and at the same time new entries are generated in the index that will allow us to find those particular files later on.

The process of moving a piece of information from working memory to long-term memory is called encoding. Encoding information is not just a matter of filing a fact into long-term memory. It is actually a dialogue between working memory and long-term memory. Before we encode a new piece of information, we first have to assign it to a mental folder or category. To do that, we must determine what parts of our existing memory are most closely related to this new information. Our prior knowledge of the topic at hand forms a context for this new knowledge currently sitting in working memory. Our prior knowledge is like a folder that already contains relevant documents, notes, images, and so on. In order to file a new piece of information in that folder, we have to take that folder out, look through the contents, and verify that it is indeed the appropriate folder in which to file this new information. Looking over the information already in the folder and analyzing the new document from our working memory creates a dialogue in our heads between what we already know and what we are just now learning. Once our minds have placed the new document into the existing file folder, it has been encoded.

Recalling Information

Remembering a piece of information is called recall, and the index entries that help us find that data are called recall cues because they prompt our memories to recall information. This indexing process is crucial. A single bit of information might have multiple recall cues. Everything we know about George Washington might be filed under both "History—American history—U.S. presidents" and "Legends involving cherry trees" or "People who had wooden teeth." Each of those recall cues can point us to what we remember about George Washington. The more index entries we have about a particular subject, the easier it is to find the appropriate file—that is, the easier it is to recall information about that subject. This is also important because over time, recall cues can be forgotten, just as index entries can be smudged or torn, and even completely crumble to dust.

But the process of encoding doesn't stop there. Our minds are skeptical clerks. They won't feel completely comfortable with how this information is filed away until it has been brought out for inspection multiple times. This process is called rehearsal, and it is the reason we review material in class. When we review old information, we are training the brain by assuring it that this piece of information belongs in this folder. The more we retrieve a fact within a certain folder, the more confident our brain clerks are that this information truly belongs here and is filed appropriately—and the faster and better we become at recalling it.

> *Our minds are skeptical clerks. They won't feel completely comfortable with how this information is filed away until it has been brought out for inspection multiple times. This process is called rehearsal, and it is the reason we review material in class.*

When we rehearse material, we have two recall methods: cued recall and free recall. Cued recall often asks a student to fill in the blank, such as "What is 5×5?" or "In what year did Christopher Columbus land in the Americas?" These questions provide cues to the answer and generate a conditioned response: 25. 1492. Tere's nothing wrong with this kind of recall, and a great volume of information needs to be memorized in this manner. Math, spelling, grammar, and playing musical scales all rely on that kind of cued recall.

Free recall, on the other hand, requires students to dig into their archives and explain what's in there without being prompted for specific facts.

For example, if I ask my biology students, "The mitochondria is the _____ of the cell?" I'm giving them a cue. They will all be able to say "powerhouse." But if I ask them to "tell me the most important things that we have learned about mitochondria," their answers will be very different. Sure, they may say it's the powerhouse of the cell, but hopefully they will supply additional information that they picked up from our study. They'll start providing a narrative. This is a great way for me as a teacher to assess what they really know. By asking them what they remember and what's most important about this topic, I will get a much better glimpse into exactly what made it into their long-term memory.

> *Practice makes permanent, not perfect—only perfect practice makes permanent perfection.*

There is both danger and beauty to this method. The danger is that if a student remembers faulty information and rehearses that in his head or if he remembers information that is not important (and fails to remember what is important), those pieces of faulty or unimportant information will latch themselves more firmly in his long-term memory. Flawed and incomplete understandings must be met with teacher or student feedback. What that means in practice is that if we are using free recall in class and a student recalls misinformation, we need to correct it quickly. And if important information is missing from a student's narrative, we need to review it quickly so that it can be encoded. If students are using this method on their own, perhaps to prepare for a test, it is crucial that they ask themselves narrative-generating questions and then check themselves against their notes or their textbook. If they do not check themselves, they run the risk of reinforcing bad information they have encoded into their long-term memories. After all, practice makes permanent, not perfect—only perfect practice makes permanent perfection.

Rehearsal

Rehearsing information helps to reinforce it. Simple repetition is helpful, at least to a certain extent. Repetition doesn't deepen our understanding or give us additional recall cues that prompt free recall. If our goal is merely to pass a test, repetition is often enough. But if our goal is transformative learning that equips us with deep understanding and robust skills, we'll need to move beyond that.

Fortunately, our brains have a built-in mechanism for moving beyond repetition of cued recall into masterful free recall. You see, the clerks in our brains are kind enough to create new index entries anytime we retrieve information in a new context. When a fifth-grader reads about George Washington for the first time in his history textbook, an initial index entry is created. But it doesn't stop there. When he has a conversation with his mother over peanut butter and jelly sandwiches at lunchtime and he makes a joke about wooden teeth and their probable impact on Washington's dietary choices, yet another entry is created. Seeing a cherry tree in full blossom and thinking about the myth of little George felling one with his new hatchet creates even more. Taking a field trip to George Washington's home, Mount Vernon, creates a whole host of new index entries. In each of those situations, information about George Washington is being retrieved, thought about, added to, filed away again, and given additional index entries.

Elaborative rehearsal is one of the most effective teaching and study methods we can impart to our students.

This process is called elaborative rehearsal. Not only are we retrieving a folder and merely reviewing its contents, but we are also elaborating on it by adding content as we review. It helps connect new information with prior knowledge and cement them all together.

Elaborative rehearsal is only one of the most effective teaching and study methods we can impart to our students. Consider another student who read the information in the textbook but did not encounter that information again except to study for the test two weeks later. His brain's volume of information and quantity of index entries would be dramatically lower than his classmate's. This means that the number of ways his mind can retrieve information about George Washington is limited. In the first case, the student has a broad working knowledge of Washington's life, accomplishments, folklore, and physical features that provides index entries in his mind right next to peanut butter and jelly, cherry trees, travel experiences, fun conversations with Mom, and a host of related index points. In the second case, however, the student's knowledge is limited and accessible only when consulting the index card entry labeled "Things I need to remember for the test." That index entry won't be rehearsed after the quiz, and it will quickly become lost, torn, or forgotten—with the end result of making all of the stored knowledge virtually inaccessible. Perhaps, given the right prodding, the second student may be able to find that file folder again later. It is not completely gone, after all. But it will be like searching for a needle in a haystack.

> *The more we think about a topic, the better we will remember it. The more opportunities we have to retrieve information from long-term memory, mix it with new information in short-term memory, file it back away, and repeat the process all over again, the better, deeper, and longer-lasting our memory of that information will be.*

This process of transferring information from sensory input through working memory and into long-term memory is neatly summed up by Dr. David Willingham in his lovely aphorism from the book *Why Don't Students Like School?*: "Memory is the residue of thought" (2009, 63). The more we think about a topic, the better we will remember it. The more opportunities we have to retrieve information from long-term memory, mix it with new information in short-term memory, file it back away, and repeat the process all over again, the better, deeper, and longer-lasting our memory of that information will be. (Of course, as mentioned earlier, we are also in danger of thinking about—and therefore remembering—incorrect information.)

You may be thinking, "That's interesting and all, but how does it help me teach?" An excellent question! There are several high-impact applications of this model.

1. Limit distractions.

Distractions come in two types: external inputs that divert our attention filter away from the most important things and internal distractions that increase our cognitive load so that our working memory can't process as much information as we need. We will deal with both sets in detail in the next chapter.

2. Limit lesson content.

Given that working memory can hold only so much information at a time, teachers should be judicious about how much information we try to pack into each lesson. We must abandon the instructional methodology that most closely resembles forcing students to drink from a firehose. Instead, our curriculum should progress through reasonable quantities of information spaced out over the course of the year.

3. Add recall cues liberally.

We should seek to make as many different connections to the information in a lesson as possible. These connections form more and stronger recall cues (our index entries). A multisensory approach will help establish a wider array of recall cues. We should also design our lessons to help students access their prior knowledge about the topic as early and as often as possible. Relating lesson materials to students' experiences helps prompt dialogue be-

> *We must abandon the instructional methodology that most closely resembles forcing students to drink from a firehose. Instead, our curriculum should progress through reasonable quantities of information spaced out over the course of the year.*

tween working and long-term memory. Unit studies tend to be particularly good at helping students connect information from multiple disciplines and access prior knowledge effectively. For example, a unit study about ancient Egypt might involve history, geography, literature, art, religion, math, and science all woven together.

EFFECTIVE STUDY SKILLS

Another crucial way that teachers and parents can help our kids is teaching them how to study material properly on their own. To do this, we need to expose bad habits for what they are and to replace them with beneficial habits.

One of the worst habits that students can build is cramming for a test. The practice is common, and for very good reason: it helps them pass tests. Unfortunately, it fails to help students learn material in a long-term, meaningful manner. Essentially, cramming piles knowledge into a file folder and creates one index entry for all of that information. That index entry is given top priority and stays at the forefront of the student's mind—but only until it is no longer required. Clearly, this is a subpar outcome.

> *Cramming is horrifically inefficient at creating long-term memories, but spaced study enables students to develop recall cues that last.*

Instead, we should teach students to space their study sessions and to use them as opportunities to create new index entries rather than simply drilling themselves on the same old index entry over and over again. "Spaced" means that there is a time gap between study sessions. Cramming is horrifically inefficient at creating long-term memories, but spaced study enables students to develop recall cues that last. The time gaps between study sessions should reflect the length of time the material should be retained. Wider gaps lead to more long-term recall (provided the gaps are not so long that students forget the material between sessions). This is why many curricula include test questions that go all the way back to the first lesson.

The more frequently information is rehearsed, the easier it becomes to recall it again. If memory is indeed the residue of thought and study sessions make information recall easier, then at a certain point, study sessions no longer involve thinking, just repetition. This is the point where students who really have mastered material tend to get frustrated. Reviewing material that they already know by heart over and over again doesn't require additional thought and therefore doesn't create stronger or better memories. There is a sweet spot between building stronger memories and reviewing ad nauseam. That is what we are aiming for.

> *We should encourage free recall, rather than just cued recall. The beauty of this method is that it makes studying much faster and more efficient.*

Further, we should encourage free recall, rather than just cued recall. The beauty of this method is that it makes studying much faster and more efficient. If after recalling all relevant pieces of information, students review their notes and confirm that their memories were correct, they can feel assured that they have indeed mastered the material. They can also quickly identify what pieces of information were missing and review them. This means that students do not necessarily need to review every single piece of material every time they study. They can limit their future reviews to those areas where they struggle to remember important details.

We teachers can build these kinds of reviews into our lesson plans. We can also teach our students about effective versus ineffective methods of studying. Helping our students move beyond parrot-like recitation of cued facts and into deep understanding of the material that allows them to collaborate, synthesize, ask questions, and explain on their own will set them up for success—and not just academically.

In the next chapter we will discuss concentration, focus, and distractions. While the material that we have discussed in this chapter applies almost universally to all students, the next chapter will invite us to consider our students' more individualized needs.

KEY POINTS

▷ Our three memory banks are sensory memory, working memory, and long-term memory.

▷ Information moves from working memory to long-term memory through a dialogue between new and prior knowledge.

▷ The more sensory connections and prior knowledge connections we make, the easier it will be to recall new information in the future.

▷ Cued recall = fill-in-the-blank. Free recall = essay question. Spaced, free-recall sessions with immediate feedback are one the most effective strategies for studying material.

CHAPTER 2

THE POWER OF

CONCENTRATION

COGNITIVE FACTORS

In the last chapter we talked about multiple ways of limiting distractions. We saw that there are two different categories of distractions: internal distractions that increase cognitive load and external distractions that make it difficult for attention filters to allow the right information into working memory. Let's dig into both of those kinds of distractions a little bit further.

As we saw in the last chapter, working memory is one of the three memory banks. When we talk about having something on our minds, we mean that something is in our working memory. Working memory has a limited capacity. We can hold only so much information in our heads at once. How much information that is varies from person to person and is a matter of debate and research among cognitive scientists.

The amount of working memory that is currently in use is called cognitive load. If the cognitive load is low, the brain is free to engage with additional information. If the cognitive load is high, we may not be able to process any new information; or if we do, it will be at the cost of other information currently in working memory. To make room for something new, we will have to flush something else that we are thinking about out of working memory.

We can break down cognitive load into two categories: effective load and ineffective load. Effective load is how much of our mental processing power is devoted to the task at hand. Ineffective load is how much of our mental processing power is devoted to thinking about things that distract us from the task at hand. For example, while reading about George Washington, I may mull over the fact that he served for only two terms, even though there was no presidential term limit at the time. That is effective load. I may also be noticing the fact that I am hungry, most likely because I failed to eat a nutritious breakfast this morning. That thought is ineffective load.

Herding Elephants

One of our goals as teachers is to minimize ineffective load (distractions) and maximize effective load. Making sure that our kids have their needs met is a simple (though not always easy way) of minimizing an effective load. Maslow's hierarchy of needs is helpful here. Abraham Maslow was a psychologist who theorized that humans have various needs that can be met only if certain prerequisite needs are met first. The base of the pyramid rests upon physiological needs such as air, food, sleep, water, and shelter. Higher-order needs like safety, meaningful relationships, the respect of others, and so on are of little import to someone who is starving or drowning.

Maslow's Heirarchy of Needs

SELF-ACTUALIZATION

ESTEEM

LOVE & BELONGING

SAFETY

PHYSIOLOGICAL

This makes intuitive sense in a teaching context: Bodily needs (if present) will always take up some amount of space in our working memory. A student who has to go to the bathroom, is hungry or thirsty, or is simply too tired has little chance of maintaining a high effective cognitive load.

Even if basic shelter and safety needs are met, higher-order needs such as relational needs may also cause ineffective load. Strained relationships with parents, siblings, friends, or others can be very distracting. As much as possible, we should strive to address those issues before we begin teaching.

> *Sometimes zoology has to wait. The elephants in the room need to be herded out the door before we can pay attention to the ones in the textbook.*

Cognitive load can be increased by many things. In a large classroom setting, it is virtually impossible to know what is on all of the students' minds at any given time. And even if we do know, we may not be able to do much about it. However, in a small classroom or a homeschool, the case is somewhat different. As a parent, knowing what is on my kids' minds may still be a challenge, but nobody is in a better position to know than I am. If I am teaching my daughter zoology and our lesson on large mammals is going nowhere because of an unkind remark a friend made, a grief that she is processing, or an argument that she and I had earlier that day, I can pause the lesson and help her process those emotions before continuing. Sometimes zoology has to wait. The elephants in the room need to be herded out the door before we can pay attention to the ones in the textbook.

I'm sure most of us have experienced something that has been difficult to handle emotionally and that has made it difficult to focus on our work. There are times when a stiff upper lip just doesn't cut it. And if we adults, who are more emotionally mature than our children, still have that experience, then we should be exceedingly gracious when our kids have that experience. Use these opportunities to help your children process their thoughts and feelings. Help them learn *how* to process thoughts and feelings. That is a skill that frequently goes untaught but is a crucial part of growing into an emotionally healthy adult. Take advantage of those learning opportunities. Your lesson plan will still be there when you come back to it.

Balancing Cognitive Load

Maximizing effective load requires us to teach engaging lessons that challenge our students and spur them to think. The more they think, the more they will learn and remember. However, there is a catch. Because working memory is limited, it can be very easy to overload our students' working memories. When cognitive load—even effective cognitive load—becomes too high or too heavy, the lesson can't be absorbed into long-term memory.

> *Often what is mistaken as a lack of character, discipline, or focus is simply the limitation of a child's brain to absorb large quantities of information.*

If they receive too much information at once, our students will shut down, remember things inaccurately or incompletely, or simply be unable to follow. Perhaps they have already flushed out foundational information upon which the rest of the lesson is built. When your students are unable to repeat instructions back to you, fidgeting, seeming like they are unable to pay attention, or not following your train of thought, it may simply be that you have exceeded their cognitive load. Often what is mistaken as a lack of character, discipline, or focus is simply the limitation of a child's brain to absorb large quantities of information.

Not every task takes up the same amount of working memory. Memorizing a list of terms is more likely to cause overload than reading a fun book. Answering a set of matching questions requires less cognitive effort than mentally rotating a 3-D diagram or finding the answer to a convoluted story problem. It is perfectly fine to use a mix of high-load and low-load activities, provided that in all cases the student is expected to engage with, think about, and process the material. Wide exposure does not produce learning if thought is not required. It really is the thought that counts. High-intensity topics tend to require more thought and lead to stronger memories, as long as working memory is not overloaded. Simply watching a video about a topic requires very little thought, unless accompanied by reflection, discussion, application, or evaluation.

If we want our students to absorb, remember, and use a large amount of information, we need to make it easy for them to remember. For example, if I give you a string of 16 digits to remember, you will likely have a very hard time repeating them back to me more than a minute later. Within an hour, that string of information will probably be flushed out. However, if I break those 16 digits down into four groups of four numbers each, you are much more likely to be able to remember them and repeat them back to me. This is why, for instance, credit card numbers are usually read over the phone and printed on the card in groups of four. Likewise, telephone numbers are not written as a single string of ten digits. We read them as a three-digit area code, followed by a set of three digits and a set of four digits. It's much easier for our minds to remember those groups. Why is that? Instead of remembering each individual number, our brains will remember the groups of numbers. This is called chunking. Rather than taking up three or four slots in our limited amount of working memory, each chunk takes up only one slot. This phenomenon is part of what enables memory masters to perform incredible feats such as memorizing multiple decks of cards and repeating all of their orders perfectly. Rather than remembering each card in each deck, memory masters remember groups of cards, and then further chunk those groups of cards into whole decks.

> *If we want our students to absorb, remember, and use a large amount of information, we need to make it easy for them to remember.*

To be even more concrete, let's say I want my students to memorize all of the countries of Africa. A list of over 50 nations would be very difficult for them to process. However, if I were to break down that list by region or some other factor into groups of five to nine countries, it would be much easier to remember all of them. Memorizing all the countries of Africa is not an unreasonable task for a junior high or high school student. But without breaking them down into groups, students' cognitive load will limit their ability to memorize. Many of us (and many students) do this naturally, even unintentionally; however, it should be taught as a skill.

Further, as we create our lesson plans, we should do our best to chunk material into meaningful groups for the students. This may involve creating mnemonic devices, such as "Kings Play Cards On Fat Green Stools" to help cue biological taxonomy terms: Kingdom, Phylum, Class, Order, Family, Genus, Species. Bruce Wilkinson, in his phenomenal work *The Seven Laws of the Learner,* calls this kind of preparation making material "mind-easy" for students (1992, 243).

ENVIRONMENTAL FACTORS

Now that we've examined some of the cognitive factors that may be limiting our students' ability to concentrate, let's take a look at some of the noncognitive factors. It is at this point that we run into two of the most famous researchers of learning styles in the last hundred years. Drs. Rita and Kenneth Dunn, a husband-and-wife researcher/educator team, proposed a model of learning styles that gained a great deal of traction in education. One portion of Dunn and Dunn's work concerned tailoring a child's learning environment to his environmental preferences in order for optimal learning to occur. They considered factors such as air temperature, lighting, background noise, and so on.

As mentioned in the introduction, the scientific studies on this and other models of learning styles are frequently inconclusive and contradictory. As with all models of learning styles, Dunn and Dunn's ideas have garnered a great deal of criticism. One criticism directed toward this approach is that it would be inexcusably expensive for public schools to attempt to implement classroom design based on students' learning preferences around the country—a concern that tends not to apply in a homeschool environment. In my opinion, their theory is worth investigating and experimenting with at home.

Some of the environmental factors considered by Dunn and Dunn are very easy to gauge at home. For instance, the first factor is whether a student prefers silence or some kind of background noise as he studies. For example, my mother, Maggie Hogan, is so hypersensitive to noise that if two conversations are occurring at the same time within earshot, she is hardly able to pay attention to either of them. When I was growing up, I frequently watched movies on mute with subtitles to avoid disturbing her, even from several rooms away. My brother, JB, on the other hand, relied on music for effective studying. As you might expect, my mother was incredulous, so my brother persuaded her to try an experiment. She would allow him to listen to his music (with headphones, of course), and at the end of the term they would see if there had been any negative impact on his grades or if his homework had taken significantly longer than usual to accomplish. The result of the experiment was that my brother was permitted to continue to listen to music while studying. His environmental preference did not match our mother's. But that was okay. As for myself, I find that background noise such as nature sounds, the hustle and bustle of a coffee shop, or instrumental music is very helpful in maintaining concentration while I work.

A second environmental preference is the relative orderliness of the workspace. I get much more done during my workday when I start by making sure I have a tidy desk and workspace than if I allow papers, letters, and other items to clutter my desk while I work. On the other hand, some people prefer creative chaos or organized chaos. A reasonable litmus test for determining whether a student's workspace is organized chaos or simply chaos is asking the student to find a particular item. If he can retrieve it within one minute, it is organized chaos. The organizational system may not look like yours, but that does not mean it is nonexistent. Those who work best in order should be encouraged and or required to keep their workspace orderly. But those who do not work well when things are too orderly should be allowed to determine their optimal level of organization.

Environmental factor number three is lighting. If the light is too bright or glaring, it may be distracting, make glossy pages unreadable, or simply make some students uncomfortable. If the light is too dim, they may have trouble reading or focusing on their pages. Some people also have preferences for warm or cool white light. Light bulbs come in a wide array of color signatures—some mimicking daylight and some with a warm, yellowish or orangish glow. Allowing students to pick out the bulbs for their desk lamps or bedroom lighting is a small thing that can give them a sense of autonomy and ownership of their learning, which is an important part of motivation. (We'll discuss that further in chapter 3.)

A fourth thing to consider is air temperature. Some people have an internal thermostat that makes it harder for the brain to function if the temperature goes above or below a certain point. If your child frequently complains about being too hot or too cold, don't ignore those complaints. A schoolchild once defined a sweater as "what my mother makes me wear when she feels cold." It is easy for parents to conflate our temperature preferences with our children's temperature preferences. If your house suffers from thermostat wars, my recommendation is to err on the side of cold air and let those who prefer warmer air put on sweaters. Those of us who prefer the cold air can do only so much to lower our temperature. Of course, don't break the bank over your utility bills.

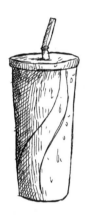

Yet another factor to consider is the presence or absence of food and drink. Students who want to have water available should always be allowed to do so. Those who like to snack while they study should be given something to munch on. (There's a list of good brain food in the appendix if you need some suggestions.) Obviously, you don't want to spoil their supper, and you may have specific rules regarding food. Just keep in mind that having something to drink and something to eat can make it easier for some students to concentrate.

Body position also plays a role. You may notice your children gravitating toward a specific piece of furniture or a specific location. If they want to study hanging upside down off the couch, underneath the kitchen table, or in the nest that they have made in the hall closet, that's fine. Some people don't like to sit at a desk for any length of time, especially if they don't have a comfortable or ergonomic chair. The discipline of sitting at a desk has very limited value, both academically or in character development. Of all the battles you could fight about their study habits, this one is the easiest to acquiesce to.

Finally, some people are morning people and others are night owls. Almost all of us have specific times of day or night when we perform our best work. While it is not always possible to accommodate teenagers who want to do all of their homework at 2:00 A.M., at least we might be able to schedule the more difficult subjects that require the most brainpower at times when they are at peak functioning ability. Fighting natural circadian rhythms is an uphill battle for anyone. Productivity is as much about managing our energy as it is about managing our time and our tasks. You might find that you or your students can get twice as much done during a morning hour than during an afternoon hour. That is something you should try to capitalize on.

A HELPFUL LEARNING ENVIRONMENT

These seven factors are worth asking your kids about. If they demonstrate strong preferences, then you may have found a simple way to reduce unwanted and unnecessary sensory input. This will allow their attention filters to focus on the most important thing: the task or lesson at hand. So take a few minutes to quiz your kids about this. Ask them to describe their ideal studying scenario. Prompt them, if needed, with questions about noise, clutter, lighting, temperature, the presence of food, the time of day, and the kind of furniture they're using. Even if you can't accommodate fully, it doesn't hurt to ask.

With all of these factors, you may find that your students have strong preferences or no preference at all. For example, I prefer to work with music; a tidy desk; cool, moving air; brightish, cool lights; water but no food; during the morning and early afternoon. When I'm operating outside my preference, it has a noticeable impact on my work output. A broken air conditioner or a cluttered desk might decrease my productivity by 50 percent. Heat, thirst, and clutter in my office all become sensory inputs that compete with my actual work for my attention, and my filter doesn't always tune things out properly—and that's to say nothing of distractions like my phone, social media, or e-mail. My wife, on the other hand, really cares only that she's warm and can see what she's working on. Other environmental factors aren't making her attention filter work overtime like they do for me. Fortunately, she is accommodating to my much more specific preferences.

My advice is that reasonable preferences should be accommodated. While I appreciate the goal of raising resilient and flexible adults, I see no reason not to allow children some control over their environment. After all, most adults have at least some level of control over our environments. Many workplaces can be very accommodating. Unless you have a very specific reason to require otherwise, these seem like small, reasonable measures that help students concentrate.

> *My advice is that reasonable preferences should be accommodated. While I appreciate the goal of raising resilient and flexible adults, I see no reason not to allow children some control over their environment.*

If, like my mother, you find your students' requests outlandish or ludicrous, I encourage you to develop an experiment like the one my brother proposed. Keep track of their grades and the amount of time spent studying both ways. If the grades stay the same or go up, there's no reason not to make environmental changes. If the time spent studying goes up, you will need to determine whether that is because they were able to spend more time studying and concentrating for longer periods of time or whether the distraction caused them to require a longer period of time to accomplish the same amount of study. Even if it took them longer to accomplish the same amount of work, if they are happier with the process and it did not prevent them from accomplishing their other responsibilities or have a negative impact on other family members, consider making the accommodation anyway. Students' enjoyment of the process of learning is often worth small sacrifices, even when inefficiencies are involved.

MULTITASKING

In addition to environmental factors, another common thief of concentration is multitasking—trying to do two things at once. Unfortunately, our brains were not designed to accommodate that. As it becomes more and more common for students to have smartphones and other devices at their fingertips while they study, or even to be studying on their computers, the temptation to multitask is almost inescapable. It is imperative for our students' learning, and future productivity that we inform them about the dangers of multitasking. The word *dangers* may sound like an overstatement, but the discipline of doing one thing at a time has much broader applications than study habits. Texting and driving can be deadly, for instance. The discipline of driving without a phone in hand is not unrelated to the discipline of studying while detached from social media and text messages.

Multitasking is more accurately termed switch-tasking because our brains are not actually doing two things at once but rather are switching back and forth between two tasks. The problem is that each switch has a cost in terms of mental energy. This is easily illustrated through the following exercise, which I encourage you to do with your children. All it requires is a stopwatch.

Time yourself as you recite all of the letters of the alphabet, from A to Z, and then the numbers 1 through 26. Stop the stopwatch and note your time. Time yourself as you again recite the alphabet and the numbers 1 through 26, but this time force yourself to say a letter and then a number, a letter and then a number, all the way until you reach "Z, 26." Note the time. Chances are that when you had to switch back and forth between the alphabet task and the number task, your time was 50 percent longer (or worse) than when you performed one task at a time. If you record yourself or write down these lists instead of saying them out loud, you may also find that you made several mistakes the second time around.

> *Multitasking is more accurately termed switch-tasking because our brains are not actually doing two things at once but rather are switching back and forth between two tasks. The problem is that each switch has a cost in terms of mental energy.*

I don't think that policing our children's multitasking is generally the best way to handle this issue. But I do think that we owe it to our kids to teach them that multitasking is essentially shooting themselves in the foot. Lives are not on the line with study habits as they are with driving, so if they are willing to accept having less discretionary time because they inflated their need for study time through multitasking, that's their choice.

KEY POINTS

▷ Working memory holds a very limited amount of information at a time. Don't overload it!

▷ Ineffective load (wasted working memory) can be caused by internal or external factors. Deal with those as best you can before digging into new material.

▷ Environmental preferences vary from person to person. To reduce distraction, make students feel comfortable while they learn whenever possible.

▷ Multitasking slows us down and causes errors.

CHAPTER 3

THE POWER OF

MOTIVATION

INTRINSIC MOTIVATION

In his excellent book *Drive: The Surprising Science of What Motivates Us*, Daniel Pink talks about the two different kinds of motivation: extrinsic and intrinsic. Extrinsic motivation is the traditional carrot-and-stick methodology that attaches rewards to good behaviors and punishments to bad ones. This sort of motivation is excellent at producing compliant workers who do exactly what is asked of them—no more and no less. It requires a strong system of managerial oversight. While this sort of motivation worked well when most jobs required the minimal creative flow of a factory assembly line, in today's economy where robots do the menial jobs and humans have to work creatively, it simply doesn't work anymore.

The second kind of motivation is intrinsic motivation, which wells up inside us rather than coming from an external system of rewards and threats. Intrinsic motivation fosters creativity, problem solving, innovation, and exploration in a way that no carrot or stick ever could. Intrinsic motivation has three key components that form the foundation for self-motivated students and workers: autonomy, mastery, and purpose.

Autonomy is critical. As any parent of teenagers knows, the struggle for independence is real. It's not a bad thing; it's just part of growing up. We were designed to take responsibility for our lives and well-being and to chafe when authority oversteps its bounds and becomes tyranny. Daniel Pink lists four areas that matter to workers and students when it comes to autonomy: task, time, team, and technique. The more we can control what we are working on (task), when we work on it (time), with whom we work (team), and how we achieve the goal (technique), the more autonomous we are and the happier we are with our work.

As teachers who want to develop lifelong, independent learners, we should keep this in mind while we plan our lessons. Can we offer our students any amount of autonomy in their work? Almost always. We may have to limit their range of choices, but we can still offer choices. Let them pick the kind of project or the topic. Let them set their own schedule as long as they meet the deadlines. Let them team up or work independently. Remember that they will learn more by using their own technique (however

> *The more we can control what we are working on (task), when we work on it (time), with whom we work (team), and how we achieve the goal (technique), the more autonomous we are and the happier we are with our work.*

inefficient) than they will if you micromanage their every move. This is especially crucial for older students, but it's also true for younger ones. Of course, sometimes there simply are constraints that they have to work with because of the nature of the assignment, the circumstances of the family, and sometimes the tolerance of the teacher. Autonomy doesn't mean that the students direct the entire lesson plan.

The second component of intrinsic motivation is mastery—the human drive to get better at something. Everyone wants to be good at something. Seeing that we have made progress in developing a skill excites us. And while we don't expect all our students to become world-class practitioners of every skill we teach them, we do expect them to grow. It is not important that they be the best, but it is important that they do better than they did last time. We need to think about the kinds of tasks that we give to our students. Do they offer our students opportunities to grow in different areas of their lives? Do they offer an appropriate level of challenge—not too easy but not too hard? Rote repetition and dry recitation of material that has been frequently rehashed offer no refreshing joys of mastery. A worksheet is convenient, but it does not provide the same kind of arena for growing skills as writing a research report, building a working model, or recreating a recipe. A little novelty and a little connection with other parts of their lives, their interests, and their goals can go a long way.

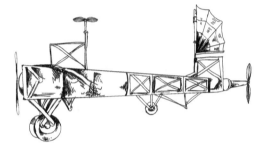

The third component of intrinsic motivation is purpose—a sense that we are part of something greater and grander than ourselves. It is a basic human need. When students fail to see any purpose or point in their studies, it is almost impossible to motivate them. Students need to understand why what they're studying matters. They need the big picture. And they need us to be honest and genuine with them. Sometimes the best reason we can muster is "because it is required if you want to graduate." But most often we can do much better than that.

Some students will be satisfied knowing that studying history or philosophy will help them become better, more well-rounded individuals or perhaps knowing that algebra stretches their mental muscles and develops their logical-mathematical intelligence. Some might even accept that studying subjects they don't like builds character. However, most students will respond better if we can provide them with concrete, real-world applications. As much as possible, your choice of activities should reflect and reinforce real-world utility. Algebra students should make the connection between solving for X and figuring out if their car will run out of gas before the next exit, assuming the next gas station is X miles away and their car gets Y miles per gallon and there are Z gallons in the gas tank. English composition students should hear from employers about the importance of a well-written cover letter and proper spelling on a résumé. Industry students should learn why they should never put out a grease or electrical fire with water. Even activities that don't appear to have a direct connection to life beyond the classroom should at least be shown to have a direct connection to the goals of the class, which in turn provides real-world benefits.

MODALITIES: PREREQUISITES OR PREFERENCES?

At this point, you may be thinking, "That's interesting, but isn't this book about learning styles?" It is, so let's explore another learning style theory that's deeply connected to these principles of motivation: the Visual, Auditory, and Kinesthetic modality model (or VAK for short). When most people talk about "learning styles," they're talking about VAK. These learning modalities have become so commonplace and entrenched in popular understanding of education that many of us can quickly and easily identify our own learning modalities and probably even the modalities of some of our children.

VAK makes a lot of sense. It's intuitive. And it suggests that if we can simply match our instructional methods to our children's learning styles or modalities, they will be able to learn better. Unfortunately, as lovely and simple an idea as that is, the science just isn't there to support that notion. I hate to be the one to burst your bubble, but you deserve to know. There isn't enough evidence in the scientific literature to demonstrate that matching instruction to students' preferred learning styles—a process known as mapping—results in higher academic achievement.

> *There isn't enough evidence in the scientific literature to demonstrate that matching instruction to students' preferred learning styles—a process known as mapping—results in higher academic achievement.*

Researchers have pointed out that to scientifically prove the mapping hypothesis, very specific tests need to be undertaken and only a certain set of results could be counted as evidence that mapping makes a positive difference in achievement (Pashler, McDaniel, Rohrer, and Bjork 2008). While the literature on learning styles is voluminous, there have been very few studies that meet the test criteria, and these studies do not demonstrate that mapping passes the test. Sometimes, mapping can produce worse results, as students may not put in enough effort to learn if the material seems easy (Salomon 1984).

If that's the case, you might ask, why even discuss modalities? The answer is easy. While mapping doesn't result in higher academic achievement per se, it does result in increased student motivation. It's not hard to see the connection between motivation and achievement. Motivated students are more likely to put effort into practicing a skill or learning material. If they spend enough time practicing the right things in the right ways, that may result in higher academic achievement. However, there are too many variables for us to safely claim that mapping alone is the key to increasing student performance.

Increasing Engagement

For example, consider a study from the University of the West of England that attempted to find ways to engage elementary students in a school building project. The school wanted to renovate some of its outdoor space and was looking for feedback from students. These researchers were concerned that conventional methods of getting feedback from the students were producing low engagement. They suspected that a multimodal approach to gathering student feedback would more deeply engage students.

In particular, they wanted to see whether different activities would elicit higher engagement rates from students, so they gave 151 students a child-friendly learning-style assessment that helped categorize the students as either visual, auditory, or kinesthetic learners. They then gave all of the students three activities to perform over the course of a few days. The first was a photo safari. Students were also given space to write down any thoughts about the pictures that they took. In the second activity, the children were placed in small discussion groups where they could give verbal feedback on

the pictures they took. These discussions were recorded, and the length of time each child spoke was measured. A final activity involved giving each child a GPS tracking device that allowed the researchers to track their movements during recess on school grounds, which would show them what areas of the school grounds children would gravitate toward.

The results of the study were fascinating. Students who identified as visual learners took 20–30 percent more photos than auditory or kinesthetic learners. Kinesthetic learners were found to have traveled on average about 70 percent further than either their visual or auditory peers. In the discussion groups, auditory learners spoke almost 50 percent longer than visual learners and nearly 90 percent longer than kinesthetic learners. There was no significant difference between boys and girls either in the results or in the distribution of learning styles (Akplotsyi and Mahdjoubi 2011). Clearly, these researchers hit upon something in their hypothesis. By providing ways for each group of learners to engage in the project with their preferred learning style, the school got more and better data for their renovation project. It is important to note that these statistically significant results do not measure anything related to academic achievement. They only reveal that preferred learning styles impact engagement with different kinds of activities. In this case, mapping resulted not in higher grades but rather in higher engagement.

Mapping and Flexing

When we map, we are essentially helping our students to feel more engaged by giving them projects and assignments they are more likely to want to do. That's it. A well-mapped assignment reduces students' ineffective cognitive load by preventing negative thoughts about the assignment itself. In some cases, particularly with kinesthetic learners, this is a huge need.

While there may be rare exceptions—especially in cases of developmental delays or learning disorders—all of us are capable of learning information presented in any modality. This is a bit startling for some of us. Many of us have grown up thinking we can only learn in one particular way. However, that idea is far more self-fulfilling prophecy than it is a neurological limitation.

This is good news for teachers. For those of us stressed out about trying to map the assignments of five children with diverse modalities, it is a relief to know that even when we do not map, our children can still learn.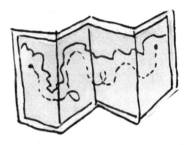

This is why we are examining what is probably the most well-known and popular learning styles theory in a chapter about motivation. Our learning modalities are tools that can help motivate us. We all have natural inclinations toward certain kinds of activities, whether they be verbal or visual, tactile or auditory. And we can use those inclinations to advantage both in ourselves and in our students. But these inclinations are not masters over us; they are servants. (In fact, I think it is more accurate to call them learning preferences rather than learning styles.)

So how should we use children's learning preferences? I offer these two rules of thumb. First, if a child is demotivated in a particular area or subject, match your instruction to his learning style as much as possible to minimize the roadblock of demotivation. If students are already struggling to even engage, we should do what we can to alleviate that struggle. Let them struggle with the material, not with their motivation.

Second, it is good for students to exercise their brains by learning some material outside of their preferred modality. This is particularly true in subjects where a student is already highly motivated or gifted. Let's examine that further.

The opposite of mapping is flexing: deliberately teaching students using a nonpreferred modality. Flexing prepares our children for future environments that are not conducive to their learning preferences. Their future professors or employers most likely will not care what their modalities are, so they should already be armed with methods to help them study material presented in nonpreferred modalities.

Additionally, flexing can force learners to slow down and engage with material more deeply. Some students with natural giftings and talents may fly through certain subjects without thinking very hard because they're just good at them. This is problematic because the moment when learning becomes difficult for them, they may fall apart, lose interest, or worse. As we have already noted, memory is the residue of thought. If students fly through the material without thinking, how can we call that learning? By forcing them to flex and use a nonpreferred learning modality, we might make the material more difficult for them, maybe even cause them to struggle. In that struggle, however, they will think; and that thinking turns into memory. We learn far more through struggle than we do through ease. There is value in struggling.

> *If students fly through the material without thinking, how can we call that learning? By forcing them to flex and use a nonpreferred learning modality, we might make the material more difficult for them, maybe even cause them to struggle. In that struggle, however, they will think; and that thinking turns into memory.*

Whether we want to map or flex, we do need to keep in mind that some subjects have inherent modality requirements. Music will always have an auditory element. Geometry is inescapably visual. Physics labs and physical education entail a kinesthetic component. Even if we wanted to map as much as possible for a highly demotivated student, there is only so much we can do. And that's OK.

> *It is worth noting that some students emphasize the need for certain kinds of input, while others emphasize particular forms of output. This distinction is sometimes referred to as receptive style versus expressive style.*

Therefore, in subjects in which your children have low initial motivation, using their leaning modality preference can give them a leg up. However, it's also worthwhile to use nonpreferred modalities for subjects that either require them or in which students already have intrinsic motivation so that they can learn to flex and meet requirements of life and higher learning.

TEACHING EACH MODALITY

The VAK Modalities

Now that we have aligned our expectations with reality, let's discuss the individual modalities and helpful teaching strategies for each. The visual, auditory, and kinesthetic modalities represent distinct ways in which students can receive, process, and communicate information.

It is worth noting that some students emphasize the need for certain kinds of input, while others emphasize particular forms of output. This distinction is sometimes referred to as receptive style versus expressive style. Among multimodal students—those who have more than one strong style preference—it is even common to display a strong preference for one kind of input and a different kind of output. For example, one student might need to see the information—receptive style—but also need to talk it out and discuss it with the teacher—expressive style. My hypothesis is that our input preferences relate more strongly to the disposition of our attention filter to let in certain kinds of information, and our expressive styles have more to do with how our working memory encodes data into long-term memory.

Let's take a brief look at each modality now. I'll provide some tools, techniques, and tips for engaging each kind of learner most effectively.

Visual

Visual learners are most engaged when they can see, watch, or read something. They tend to form strong mental pictures. Give them plenty of visual stimuli in a variety of forms. Well-illustrated books, posters, PowerPoint presentations, concept maps, handouts, flowcharts, and diagrams all give visual learners something to latch on to. Encourage them to take notes—not just in words but also in pictures, comics, diagrams, or even doodles. Let them—or rather ask them to—color, draw, and illustrate what they're hearing while they listen to lectures. Translating verbal information into visual information is a great exercise for them, and it gives you a good window into their understanding and feelings about the material. Help them to become aware of the pictures in their minds; those mental images become a significant part of what is encoded into long-term memory.

Tools and Techniques: Visual

1. Making flashcards, challenge cards, and other picture-oriented tools for review

2. Making illustrations of events, concepts, objects, or people

3. Making maps

4. Labeling diagrams

5. Creating concept maps or mindmaps

6. Using graphic organizers

7. Taking field trips, both in person and virtual

8. Watching simulations and animations of processes, events, or systems

9. Reading or making designs and blueprints

10. Watching videos

11. Making models, dioramas, and replicas

12. Dramatization, with a focus on set and/or costume design

13. Painting, drawing, and sketching

14. Viewing and making charts, graphs, and infographics

15. Viewing and making timelines

16. Reading and creating comics

17. Seeing and putting on live performances

18. Making and solving puzzles

19. Tracing maps, illustrations, diagrams, and other pictures

20. Creating outlines of their own or other people's material

21. Keeping a subject notebook

22. Highlighting and underlining text in multiple colors

23. Creating PowerPoint presentations

Auditory

Auditory learners are easily mischaracterized. Some people assume that auditory learners can just absorb and understand large amounts of lecture. However, auditory input is only a part of the equation; expression is often equally important. Auditory learners need to talk, to discuss, to hear themselves say something, or even to teach the information before they feel like they have a solid grasp of it. If auditory learners can teach the information back to you or to another student and can answer questions, that's often the best indicator that they have mastered the material. Auditory learners often work best in small-group settings, which give them sounding boards. Sometimes they might have trouble with social graces like not interrupting, dominating conversations, or speaking out of turn. It's hard to blame them; they're just trying to learn. It can be hard for teachers to strike the right balance between engaging in conversation and reinforcing etiquette. The best advice I have is to enforce silence when needed but give them plenty of opportunity to talk before the lesson is over.

Auditory learners need to talk, to discuss, to hear themselves say something, or even to teach the information before they feel like they have a solid grasp of it.

Tools and Techniques: Auditory

1. Singing songs
2. Memorization and recitation
3. Group or one-on-one discussion
4. Dramatization or role-playing
5. Giving oral reports
6. Storytelling
7. Reading aloud (and being read to)
8. Debate
9. Socratic inquiry
10. Listening to lectures, seminars, or audiobooks
11. Chanting rhymes
12. Verbalizing or repeating back information they're given (especially instructions)
13. Working with a partner
14. Recording audio or video for use either as personal drills or as reports and projects
15. Writing songs about the subject (either original works or parodies of other works)
16. Reading along with audiobooks or reading subtitles on videos
17. Narrating and describing visual input like maps, charts, and diagrams
18. Rephrasing and paraphrasing

Kinesthetic

I have a soft spot for kinesthetic learners. These are the restless ones, the fidgeters, the kids with springs in their bottoms, the students who just can't sit still. It's not a disorder, disrespect, or lack of discipline. Kinesthetic learners simply have a legitimate need to move. They need to do. My belief is that these learners have attention filters that prioritize tactile and sensory input (especially from muscles that feel cramped from too much stillness) over and above most auditory and visual input and that this overabundance of physical sensory data causes high ineffective load. If this is the case, it explains why movement, stretching, and exercising seem to clear their minds. Nerves that shout "this muscle is bored and needs to do something" (ineffective load) quiet down when they move, which frees cognitive resources for the task or lesson at hand (effective load). For this reason, many effective strategies for kinesthetic learners have less to do with lesson planning and more to do with engaging their bodies so that they're not distracted by their own muscles.

> *Rather than being frustrated or overwhelmed by their abundant energy, put that energy to good use. Allow these learners to move while you're teaching them.*

Rather than being frustrated or overwhelmed by their abundant energy, put that energy to good use. Allow these learners to move while you're teaching them. Teach them that it's OK to doodle or have something quiet to fiddle with in their hands, such as Silly Putty, a Rubik's Cube, or other small toys. Let them tinker, fiddle, and mess around. As long as they can demonstrate that they're learning the material, their own preferred methods are probably OK. In circumstances where sitting still is required, at least try to take frequent breaks. Something as simple as running a lap around the house or walking around the coffee table between assignments or questions can go a long way. Some people will put their students' assignment pages on a clipboard and let kids write as they walk around the house, outside, or on a treadmill.

Tools and Techniques: Kinesthetic

1. Creating hand gestures
2. Storytelling
3. Dramatization
4. Work experience, such as jobs, apprenticeships, or internships
5. Personal mentoring
6. Making models, dioramas, and replicas
7. Hands-on experimentation and lab work
8. Replicating, reenacting, or recreating
9. Dance
10. Sewing
11. Tracking and pointing with a finger while reading
12. Drawing
13. Touching and feeling material samples, such as rocks, fabrics, tree bark and leaves, viscous liquids, etc.
14. Exercising
15. Tracing maps, illustrations, diagrams, and other pictures
16. Using manipulatives
17. Walking on visual-aid floor mats and maps
18. Taking breaks
19. Construction and assembly
20. Tinkering
21. Disassembly
22. Coloring
23. Writing things by hand
24. Movement-based music
25. Making or solving puzzles
26. Highlighting and underlining text

In 1987, Neil Fleming published a revision of VAK called the VARK® model. The added R stands for "read/write." In the VAK system, reading and writing are combined with the visual modality, whereas Fleming claims the visual modality deals primarily with maps, charts, diagrams, and other symbolic representations rather than text. A student who has a read/write preference according to VARK will prefer strategies for learning that are different from a student who has a VARK visual preference. You can read more about VARK and Fleming's work at www.VARK-Learn.com.

Teaching Multiple Modalities

While some students prefer a single strong modality, most people are multimodal, having two or more preferred modes. Some can switch from mode to mode as the occasion requires. These students make teachers' lives easier. Other students seem to want input from both or all of their preferred modes before they feel fully comfortable with the material. That can be a bit more challenging but likely will result in the deepest understanding.

Using a diversity of activities that appeal to multiple modalities is worthwhile. If we're teaching a group of any size, it's almost essential to cast a wide net, as the likelihood of an entire classroom having the same modalities is slim. Even if we're teaching only a single student, we've already seen the value of both mapping and flexing.

The ancient Hebrews approached education with multiple modalities in mind (knowingly or not, I can't say). Recall Deuteronomy 6:6–9, one of the most famous biblical passages on education:

> And these words that I command you today shall be on your heart. You shall teach them diligently to your children, and shall talk of them when you sit in your house, and when you walk by the way, and when you lie down, and when you rise. You shall bind them as a sign on your hand, and they shall be as frontlets between your eyes. You shall write them on the doorposts of your house and on your gates. (ESV, emphasis added)

I used to see this passage and think "Doesn't that seem like overkill?" Now, however, I see it as a merciful, multimodal approach that made sure children of all learning preferences would be engaged. Both mapping and flexing occurred. The auditory kids talked with their parents. The kinesthetic ones walked with their parents. The visual learners saw the signs—big ones on the door and gates and small ones on the hands and foreheads, as well as the words in front of them daily, possibly in big bold print. Everyone was covered. How kind of God to make sure all of his children were included in his lesson plan!

You may have noticed that several of the tools and techniques above were listed under multiple modalities. Activities and tools such as dramatization, making folderbooks, and map work are efficient means of casting a wide net. For example, the process of filling out outline maps using an attractive atlas as a reference will naturally appeal to visual learners; auditory learners will want to discuss what they're seeing or reading; and kinesthetic learners can trace the route of Marco Polo or Jonah with their fingers.

Tying It All Together

By understanding the building blocks of motivation in combination with learning modalities, you will be able to more effectively engage your students in the learning process. Providing assignments that map to their modality (or at least a choice of assignments, some of which map to their learning modality) is an easy way to increase autonomy. If mapped assignments have a sufficient level of challenge, they increase the mastery component. Conversely, work that forces students to flex their modalities can appeal to the mastery element as well, as long as assignments are not overly difficult. Flexing is also a great opportunity to emphasize purpose.

Carrots and sticks, gold stars and dunce caps simply do not motivate. At least, they do not produce the kinds of creative, independent, innovative learners that the world needs today. As Plutarch said, "The mind is not a vessel that needs filling, but wood that needs igniting" (1992, 50). The more we can provide our students with autonomy, opportunities for mastery, and a sense of purpose, the stronger their intrinsic motivation will be.

KEY POINTS

▷ Extrinsic motivation (carrots and sticks) works only for dull, repetitive tasks. Intrinsic motivation (mastery, autonomy, and purpose) is required for everything else.

▷ Learning modalities are preferences, not prerequisites. They predict engagement, not achievement.

▷ Visual, auditory, and kinesthetic learners are more likely to fully engage in different kinds of activities.

▷ Mapping is best for areas in which students are already demotivated. Flexing is useful for building skills and challenging them in areas where they're already motivated or talented.

Chapter 4

The Power of

Growth

What Is Intelligence?

In the previous chapters, we've discussed the process of learning that everyone experiences, and we've looked at individual preferences in connection with concentration and motivation. We have also highlighted the fact that modalities and environmental factors are preferences rather than requirements.

In this chapter, we're going to look at a learning style theory that can impact your lesson planning, your relationship with your children, and even your personal philosophy of education. This theory is Dr. Howard Gardner's theory of multiple intelligences (MI).

Dr. Howard Gardner, a psychologist, asked "What exactly does it mean to be intelligent?" as he studied developmental psychology and neuropsychology in the 1970s. Dissatisfied with the uniform view of intelligence that measured only reading, writing, and mathematics, he proposed an alternative way of understanding the mind in his 1983 landmark book *Frames of Mind: The Theory of Multiple Intelligences*. According to Gardner, there are at least nine different kinds of intelligence, each of which allows people to identify and solve different kinds of problems and each of which is localized in a different part of the brain (among other criteria).

Gardner's list includes linguistic, logical-mathematical, visual-spatial, bodily-kinesthetic, musical, naturalist, interpersonal, intrapersonal, and existential-spiritual intelligences. There may be other intelligences as well that haven't been identified yet (and there are certainly other theories and models of intelligence, but they fall outside the scope of this book). Here's a brief look at each of Gardner's intelligences and the kind of skills each one governs.

Linguistic Intelligence

Students with high linguistic intelligence enjoy reading, writing, and/or speaking. Some lean toward the written word, others toward the spoken. This "word smart" intelligence helps us appreciate poetry and literature and allows us to communicate with clarity or eloquence.

Logical-Mathematical Intelligence

"Logic smarts" are the core of our analytical reasoning capacity. This logical-mathematical intelligence allows us to use the scientific method, calculate equations, and think like a detective. Asking thoughtful questions, performing math, and following instructions are all functions of this intelligence, from simple counting to the complexities of programming a computer.

Visual-Spatial Intelligence

If you have an eye for something, it's because of visual-spatial intelligence. Interpreting diagrams, remembering pictures, rotating 3-D objects in our minds, selecting colors, and observing works of art all have their home here. This "picture smart" part of the brain helps us recognize faces, doodle in our sketchbooks, sculpt, make flowcharts, paint, take photographs, and estimate how many sets of clothes will fit inside a suitcase before it won't close. It lets us solve mazes, assemble puzzles, and pick out matching clothes.

Bodily-Kinesthetic Intelligence

Our sense of balance, speed, direction, and touch all belong to bodily-kinesthetic intelligence. Athletes, gymnasts, dancers, jugglers, and actors as well as builders, sculptors, drivers, and many other occupations rely on this kind of "body smart." If a skill relates to movement, balance, athleticism, dexterity, hand/eye coordination, or other motor skills—gross or fine—it's part of this intelligence.

Musical Intelligence

Musical intelligence allows us to appreciate music and gives us the ability to sing, play instruments, compose and arrange, and analyze music. It lets us identify musical instruments by sound; distinguish genres; find the right note; harmonize; and vary our pitch, tone, and timbre.

Naturalist Intelligence

Naturalist intelligence governs how we observe and interact with the natural world. Survival skills like identifying plants and animals, predicting weather, orienteering, noticing patterns in nature, and all kinds of other outdoorsy activities are based on our "nature smarts." People with this intelligence often like to raise and care for animals; grow gardens; collect rocks, shells, and bugs; and play outside.

Interpersonal Intelligence

Interpersonal intelligence allows us to understand other people, empathize with them, and read between the lines from their tone and body language. Individuals with strong "people smarts" usually have solid social skills, can form positive relationships, and know how to make themselves likable. They can mediate disputes, make friends, lead groups, counsel, motivate, and persuade (or even manipulate) people, if they so desire.

Intrapersonal Intelligence

What "people smarts" are to others, "self smarts" are to ourselves. People with intrapersonal intelligence tend to be particularly good at knowing and understanding themselves. They engage in introspection and can process their thoughts and emotions. They usually know how to set goals and take care of themselves physically and mentally, and they have thought about their own personalities and gifts. Metacognition (thinking about thinking) comes easier for these folks and gives them an edge in self-improvement and reflection. They may keep journals and want to spend time alone with their thoughts.

Existential-Spiritual Intelligence

Existential-spiritual intelligence deals with philosophical thinking and grappling with life's big questions. "Life smarts" allow us to ponder the meaning of life and our place in the world, sort through moral and ethical dilemmas, and consider our spirituality. Our sense of justice, compassion, and ability to examine worldviews and religion are rooted in this intelligence. More than any other, this intelligence overlaps and influences the others, and it is the only one of Gardner's intelligences that does not have its own unique portion of the brain that governs it, leading some to call it a half-intelligence—not because it is unimportant but because intelligence may not be the right word for it.

Does this sound similar to our discussion of modalities? You may have noticed some apparent overlap between multiple intelligence theory and the VAK modalities. Visual and visual-spatial intelligence seem to match, as do auditory and linguistic intelligence, and the kinesthetic modality and bodily-kinesthetic intelligence. In fact, many people confuse the two theories.

We should be careful, however, not to conflate intelligences with modalities. Dr. Gardner himself discourages us from doing so, and for important reasons. There are crucial differences between VAK modalities and Gardner's intelligences. Modalities address the question "How do we like to learn?" They're essentially communication preferences. On the other hand, multiple intelligence theory addresses the question "What are we good at?" The nine intelligences represent ability.

ASSESSING SMARTS

If we accept that intelligence is multifaceted, how does that impact our teaching? First, it should cause us to examine our method of assessing students' achievement.

The traditional method of measuring intelligence is an IQ test. Originally pioneered in 1900 by psychologist Alfred Binet, the IQ (or Intelligence Quotient) test measured students' potential ability in mathematical reasoning and critical reading, encapsulating their life accomplishment potential into one simple number. More tests since Binet's have attempted to quantify mental acuity and academic potential. The SAT and similar tests represent an easy way to rate and rank students, and they are widely used by colleges, employers, and even the military to determine a candidate's aptness for various tasks and fields.

The problems with such an approach are manifold. Many of us resist the idea of having our potential reduced to a number. Clearly, these kinds of tests overlook a wide array of skills beyond computation and reading comprehension. Many of us know people who simply don't test well despite having deep knowledge and even wisdom; standardized tests don't serve them well. Conversely, a high test score doesn't imply a candidate has the character or personality traits needed for success in any given field. Interests, experiences, passion, and curiosity are all ignored in this testing model.

> *While two individuals may share an IQ or SAT score, no two people have the exact same intelligence profile.*

While two individuals may share an IQ or SAT score, no two people have the exact same intelligence profile. Each of Gardner's nine intelligences exists in every person in varying degrees. When we consider these kinds of intelligences, tests like the SAT that focus almost exclusively on linguistic and logical-mathematical intelligences start to show their rather narrow utility. "Word smarts" and "logic smarts" are certainly important in today's world, and they can be useful predictors of academic success. But if we want to take a holistic approach to our children's education, we should look at more than just those two factors.

There's not a standardized achievement test that covers all of the various intelligences, and that's OK. Free MI tests are available online, but the two simplest ways of assessing your child's strengths and weaknesses are observation and self-reporting. Observing your students and reflecting on those observations is an essential practice that will give you valuable insight as you seek to teach them well. Even easier is asking them what they think. If you read the list of intelligences to your students, they'll probably be able to pick out at least one or two that they recognize in themselves. You may be able to identify even more in them than they can.

MULTIPLE INTELLIGENCE LESSON PLANNING

MI theory helps us see where additional instruction, coaching, interventions, and other experiences might help shore up areas of weakness. We can't all be masters of every part of our brains, and sometimes we need to work a little harder on our trouble spots. As you look at curriculum and wade through textbooks, lesson plans, and activities, ask what intelligence(s) each experience or activity builds in your students. If a student needs to be stretched in a certain area, select activities that will build those skills.

If students are struggling with a particular skill, you can help them use other intelligences to bolster their weak points. Consider using word problems to help students who struggle with math and are more word smart. Picture-smart students may want to draw diagrams or illustrations of the problem. Musical students may want to learn or write a song to help them remember formulae or concepts like order of operations. People-smart students might do better studying with friends, quizzing each other, or playing math games in a group. I highly recommend giving your student a copy of Dr. Thomas Armstrong's book *You're Smarter Than You Think: A Kid's Guide to Multiple Intelligences*. It is a fantastic student guide on how to use and grow each kind of intelligence. It has strategies for shoring up weaknesses and capitalizing on strengths. Dr. Kathy Koch's delightful and accessible book *8 Great Smarts* is a good resource for parents.

When some people learn about Gardner's theory, they think that they have to rewrite their lesson plans to tie in to each intelligence as a sort of massive multimodal approach. I've seen impressive sample lessons that include a station for each intelligence with unique activities. Students have to use a different intelligence at each station to grapple with the material.

> *If you're making a big stretch to try to connect four additional intelligences to one lesson, you're probably overdoing it. Even if you find a connection, is it really going to help grow their skill, or are you just trying to check all the boxes?*

If you find that prospect intimidating, you're not alone. While such plans certainly have multimodal appeal, exercise more parts of the brain, and are likely to build strong memories, they also have weaknesses. For one thing, I've yet to meet a teacher or parent who has the time to develop nine different intelligence-based activities for each lesson. That sounds dramatically impractical. Second, not all subject matter has meaningful ties to every intelligence. I would have a hard time trying to find meaningful, memorable existential connections to the quadratic equation or relevant musical and linguistic activities for a lesson on volcanos. That's not to say they can't be done, but if you're making a big stretch to try to connect four additional intelligences to one lesson, you're probably overdoing it. Even if you find a connection, is it really going to help grow their skill, or are you just trying to check all the boxes?

> *I'd prefer that my students and children build confidence (and character) through the struggle of learning rather than by being thrown softballs that reinforce their favorite skills.*

Some people argue that appealing to each intelligence in our lessons gives each student a chance to shine somewhere, which keeps them motivated and builds self-esteem. I would counter that multimodal teaching already addresses motivation and that building self-esteem isn't an essential function of education. To be frank, I'd prefer that my students and children build confidence (and character) through the struggle of learning rather than by being thrown softballs that reinforce their favorite skills. There will be plenty of opportunities for them to work in each intelligence over the course of their education. As a teacher, I shouldn't feel constrained to include all nine in each lesson or even each subject.

MI at Home

In addition to adding a new dimension to our lessons, MI theory also has implications for us as parents who want to love our kids well. A simple awareness of the MI framework helps us understand our kids better. Parents and children often have a hard time understanding how and what the other person thinks. Even more important, parents sometimes do not value their children's brand of intelligence, which can lead to disappointment, frustration, and resentment on both sides. Children who want to go out for sports or dance because they delight in using their bodily-kinesthetic intelligence might encounter resistance from parents who value music, math, or reading over physical activities.

Knowing our children's intelligence strengths helps us to appreciate them more deeply—which, incidentally, is a surprisingly important aspect of helping them learn. Children who do not feel a sense of belonging, of being a valued member of their learning community (which may also be their family), are likely to feel unmotivated, have significant ineffective cognitive load (arising from negative thoughts and feelings), and thus underperform. We must show our kids that their brand of "smart" is valued, that they are valued, and that the size of their talent or ability is not the basis of their worth.

MI theory can help with communication and appreciation, but even more important, it can help us pass on one of the most powerful gifts that parents can give their children: a growth mindset. Everyone wants to be smart, but not everyone thinks they are. Many of us grew up thinking of intelligence as something fixed at birth. MI theory rejects that idea and reminds us that all of us can grow. You could say (as Salman Khan of Khan Academy does) that we can, in essence, make ourselves smarter—that intelligence is fluid, not fixed, and can benefit from mental exercise in much the same way that muscles can grow from physical exercise. Each intelligence can be developed, and new abilities can be unlocked.

Ability is an important word to define. It is sometimes used interchangeably with *skill, aptitude, talent, gifting,* and other terms leading to obfuscation. As working definitions, we will say that your ability to perform a task, grapple with a question, etc. is a combination of your natural talent (inborn giftings and inclinations) and learned skill (acquired through study and practice). In this equation, we might say that talent is nature while skill is nurture. A child prodigy like Mozart was born with a great deal of natural musical talent, which was then nurtured through rigorous study and practice.

> *Those with natural talent may exceed the ability of their peers early on, but talent alone does not lead to mastery.*

Those with natural talent may exceed the ability of their peers early on, but talent alone does not lead to mastery. Through study and practice, less talented students may surpass their more talented peers who coast on their talents instead of developing their skill. Talent does not grow, but skill can. In fact, students who are willing to devote the time, energy, focus, and effort can continue to grow indefinitely. This is encouraging news for life-long learners everywhere.

THE GROWTH MINDSET

While all of us have all nine kinds of intelligence, everyone has natural propensities toward some over others. Conversely, all of us likely have one or more intelligences in which we appear to be weak. Don't be discouraged! Skill is acquired through practice. Even where talent is low, we can develop our skill if we're motivated to practice diligently. This means that we can essentially make ourselves smarter. The caveat is that it can take a lot of motivation and grit to get better if we struggle in certain areas. The limit to our improvement in any given area is usually sustaining our interest and motivation as opposed to any hardwired neurological barrier.

This is really important, so I'll repeat myself. The biggest obstacle to increasing skill in any given area is not neurological or physical; it's our mindset, our motivation, and our perseverance. If we believe that we're not really able to learn something, it becomes a self-fulling prophecy. If we quit before putting in enough time or effort, we won't get better. If we think there's no point in getting better at something, we won't. If we let our inevitable mistakes, perfectionism, or the frustration of struggling stop us from moving forward, we'll flounder.

Dr. Carol Dweck has done some fascinating research into what she calls the "fixed mindset" and the "growth mindset." A person with a fixed mindset believes that intelligence is essentially static and that some people simply have more than others. People with a growth mindset, by contrast, believe that they can improve their abilities through hard work, good teaching, and persistence. We may not grow to the level of Einstein, Mozart, or Milton in their various strengths, but we can certainly be better today than we were last week.

While most students won't verbalize either of those mindsets, their reactions to failure or setbacks can be a good indicator of where they stand. If failure cripples them, or if they shrug it off because "I'm not good at X," that's a fixed mindset at work. Seeing failure as just a setback, an opportunity for growth, or simply a case of "I haven't solved this problem yet" indicates a growth mindset. Incidentally, Dweck notes that praising children for their intelligence ("You're so smart!") tends to foster a fixed mindset, while praising kids for their perseverance, methodology, or reaction to challenges and setbacks helps foster a growth mindset. (For more on this topic, see Dweck's TED Talk online or her book *Mindset*.)

Setting Smart Goals with MI

Understanding MI theory can help us understand our children (and ourselves) better, help us to develop a growth mindset, and give us strategies for shoring up weak points in our kids' education. But there's another bigger-picture application of MI theory that makes it especially useful. MI theory helps us develop our philosophy of education and informs our long-term goal-setting in accordance with our values and our children's future vocations.

Consider for a moment how different societies around the world and through history have valued certain intelligences over others. Often, these varieties of intelligence equate to survival skills. For instance, in *Frames of Mind*, Dr. Gardner describes the Puluwat islanders of Micronesia, who were noted for their advanced marine navigation techniques that relied on seafarers' knowledge of the stars, currents, weather conditions, and sailing techniques. Visual-spatial intelligence was essential for finding their way from one island to the next, along with a strong set of nature smarts and body smarts as they handled their vessels through the waters. If they failed to learn these skillsets, they could wind up dead in the water.

For contrast, consider how the wealthy Caroline Bingley (from Jane Austen's classic *Pride and Prejudice*) describes a truly accomplished woman:

> No one can be really esteemed accomplished, who does not greatly surpass what is usually met with. A woman must have a thorough knowledge of music, singing, drawing, dancing, and the modern languages, to deserve the word; and besides all this, she must possess a certain something in her air and manner of walking, the tone of her voice, her address and expressions, or the word will be but half deserved ([1813] 2001, 27).

In Jane Austen's Regency-era England, a woman's fortunes depended on marrying well. According to Miss Bingley, in order to attract a desirable husband, a lady had to demonstrate musical intelligence (singing and playing), visual intelligence (drawing), kinesthetic intelligence (dancing and graceful movement), linguistic intelligence (speaking several languages), and interpersonal intelligence (etiquette, social skills, and her "air"). Lacking these qualities, a lady might not marry well (or at all) and soon find herself dead—socially, if not literally.

Today, we can see how each intelligence has practical utility for all kinds of vocations. Builders, artists, and athletes all need kinesthetic intelligence. Counselors, clergy, and managers need intrapersonal and interpersonal intelligences. Vets, farmers, and biologists require nature smarts. Programmers, engineers, and scientists rely on logical-mathematical ability. The list could go on.

> *By understanding their strengths and weaknesses, we can give better guidance as they ponder their vocations and long-term plans.*

With all that in mind, I think one of the most useful applications of Gardner's theory is in helping us to develop strong goals and plans for our children's education. By understanding their strengths and weaknesses, we can give better guidance as they ponder their vocations and long-term plans. For example, a teenager with strong musical ability can be given additional opportunities to grow in musicianship, while also paying attention to other smarts related to their possible careers: linguistic intelligence for singer-songwriters, logical-mathematical for composers, kinesthetic (acting and dance) for the Broadway-bound singer, or interpersonal networking skills with broad utility for any musician. Vocations rarely rely on a single skill, so developing a strong base of related skills is advantageous.

What do intelligence-based goals look like? In my family, we affirm that there is both intrinsic worth and functional value in every intelligence. However, we believe that three intelligences stand out as the survival skills of our day: linguistic, logical-mathematical, and interpersonal intelligences. This is reflected in the marketplace. Job openings in every sector describe these three smarts using terms like "outstanding written and verbal communication skills," "problem-solving skills," and "team player." Aside from character traits like responsibility, integrity, and a strong work ethic, employers' most important criteria for new hires are often these three intelligences.

Almost every arena appears to have deep needs that only those three intelligences can meet. They fill consistent gaps in the marketplace, the non-profit world, at home, and in academia. Because word smarts, logic smarts, and people smarts are so particularly vital for our world today, we emphasize those three abilities in our educational choices for our children. For instance, if our son had opportunities for either a public speaking class (which develops interpersonal and linguistic skills) or piano lessons (which focus on musical and kinesthetic ability) and he had no strong personal preference or a hint of a musical career in front of him, we would almost certainly sign him up for the public speaking class. Is there value in music lessons, even for those who are not musically inclined? Absolutely. But based on our philosophy of education, we find even more value in public speaking for our kids.

You may disagree about the primacy of those skills, and that's OK. My goal in making that statement is to encourage you to think about what skills you think hold the most value and which intelligences you want most to foster in your children. Do you believe that they should all be developed equally or that certain skills should be emphasized? Perhaps you think that those decisions should be led by the student rather than enforced by the parents. I'm not here to write your philosophy of education for you, but I do you think you should consider these questions for yourself. The answers will guide you when you have to make choices about what you do and don't do with and for your kids.

You can do almost anything, but you can't do everything. A well-developed personal philosophy of education that includes goals about what skills and intelligences you most want to develop can help you make those decisions wisely. Having clear goals as part of your personal philosophy of education is important. Knowing what skills are essential will allow you to form smarter goals, get more useful data from your assessments (even informal ones), better relate with your children, and spur them on toward growth.

KEY POINTS

▷   There is more than one way to be smart.

▷   Understanding our multiple intelligences can help us appreciate
    and communicate with our students.

▷   We can grow in all of our intelligences through diligent effort,
    study, and good teaching.

▷   While we don't have to include every intelligence in every lesson,
    we should be aware of which intelligences we're developing and be
    intentional about doing so.

CHAPTER 5

THE POWER OF

CURRICULUM

EXPERIENCES

If we want to take advantage of the powers of memory, concentration, motivation, and growth that we've discussed so far, we're going to need a plan. Fortunately, such plans are readily available in the form of curricula (even if they require some tweaking).

There is no broadly accepted definition of *curriculum*. For some, it is a cumulative total of all lessons learned, academic and otherwise, intentional and coincidental. For others, it is a detailed plan of the course of instruction, topics to be covered, and standards that must be met. Some talk of curricula that encompasses many years or the whole of a student's academic career, while others refer to only a specific year's plan. Such a plan may include all disciplines, include only a subset of them, or a focus on a single subject. Colloquially, it's often used to refer to a particular textbook or package of books and other media. For our purposes, I will limit our scope and definition to an instructional plan together with its requisite books and resources covering a single year's instruction in one subject area.

In his classic book *Basic Principles of Curriculum and Instruction*, Ralph W. Tyler says that curriculum should seek to answer four questions:

1. What educational purposes should the school seek to attain?
2. What educational experiences can be provided that are likely to attain these purposes?
3. How can these educational experiences be effectively organized?
4. How can we determine whether these purposes are being attained? (1949, 1)

These four questions provide a kind of rubric that we can use in selecting curricula for our students. Does the program in question have clear goals, a variety of meaningful experiences, useful organization, and relevant assessments? If you can answer those four questions positively, you're off to a good start.

> *These four questions provide a kind of rubric that we can use in selecting curricula for our students. Does the program in question have clear goals, a variety of meaningful experiences, useful organization, and relevant assessments?*

Unfortunately, not all curricula on the market today do a good job of answering or even considering these questions. Some fail by not clearly laying out their goals. Others fail by not creatively considering the second question about experiences, instead relying on stale, boring, and dry approaches to information transmittal that generally do not promote the kind of thinking and engagement students require in order to make meaningful long-term memories. The textbook approach to education is notorious for this failure. Fortunately, more and more publishers are recognizing the value of hands-on, multimodal, and innovative experiences in instructional design. A third failing, disorganization, is often seen in programs that haven't been rigorously tested. Disorganized curriculum frequently confuses students or frustrates teachers, who find the curriculum too difficult to use effectively. Last, some programs fail to properly assess whether or not the educational goals are being attained.

EDUCATIONAL GOALS

Let's take a closer look at Ralph Tyler's first question. As parents, we hold the primary responsibility for our children's education. The buck stops with us—not with the state, a school, or any other teacher. We have the freedom to delegate some of the tasks of teaching to others (which we do whenever we avail ourselves of public or private schools, co-ops, or tutors). Even so, our children remain our own responsibility. In that sense, we supervise all their teachers.

In light of that responsibility which we undertook when we brought children into this world, it makes sense that we ought to have some idea of what our goals and guiding principles are for their education. Writing down the guiding principles behind your educational decisions and goals establishes your personal philosophy of education, while enumerating your goals is defines your curriculum (in the broad definition).

Let's talk about philosophy of education a bit more. Consider the mission statement of the U.S. Department of Education: "[The Department of Education]'s mission is to promote student achievement and preparation for global competitiveness by fostering educational excellence and ensuring equal access" (2018, emphasis added). Note the emphasis on achievement (which translates to test scores) and competitiveness (meaning job skills). An ungenerous rephrasing of that mission would be "The Department of Education exists to make sure kids learn how to take tests and get jobs." Of course, I doubt many public school teachers would claim that as their own mission (at least, not in those words), but the department's own language is still rather telling about how the federal government views the purpose of education. Contrast this with Martin Luther King, Jr.'s famous statement:

> The function of education, therefore, is to teach one to think intensively and to think critically. But education which stops with efficiency may prove the greatest menace to society. The most dangerous criminal may be the man gifted with reason, but with no morals. . . . We must remember that intelligence is not enough. Intelligence plus character—that is the goal of true education. (1947)

Quite a different picture, isn't it? As parents, we have goals for our children's education that likely include such things as moral instruction; preparation for adulthood, including social readiness and life skills; preparation for their future, whether that entails getting started in a trade or profession or identifying the right next step in their education; teaching good citizenship; etc. My family's philosophy of education statement is "We homeschool in order to help our children become life-long learners; competent adults; pursuers of truth, goodness, and beauty; and most importantly, disciples of Jesus." It reads much like a vision statement. Of course, approaches vary from family to family and child to child. Yours will almost certainly be different from mine, and that's OK.

> *"We must remember that intelligence is not enough. Intelligence plus character— that is the goal of true education."*
>
> *-Martin Luther King, Jr.*

Setting goals for the school year builds on the foundation of our philosophy of education; it is the logical next step. It helps us tie the big picture to our yearly plan as we select the subjects and textbooks we plan to use and decide which activities to prioritize. MI theory is helpful here, as we briefly discussed in the previous chapter. For example, when I was in high school, my parents placed a great deal of emphasis on pursuing our passions and interests, as well as volunteerism. They thought these efforts built character and would help me expand my interpersonal, musical, linguistic, and intrapersonal skills. As a result, I spent plenty of time in choir and orchestra, doing community service and church projects, and traveling on missions trips and with the family business. They also knew that these experiences would prompt valuable discussions and provide opportunity for reflection, which fit my auditory modality very well. While I didn't receive academic credit for all of these activities, they were an important part of my education (and most of them went on my transcript). Similarly, they chose to forego trigonometry and calculus (not required in our state at the time) in favor of personal finance and business math. They valued real-world life skills and knew that additional higher-level math would be frustrating for me, so it was an easy choice (and one that has served me well).

So "What educational purposes should the school seek to attain?" They'll vary from family to family. Your family's goals might include information about the following:

- particular subjects and content knowledge you value

- a ratio of mapping and flexing modalities

- certain skills (academic and otherwise) you wish to see mastered

- mindsets, values, and worldviews (like a growth mindset, your faith, the value of a peaceful home environment, or a work ethic) that you wish to pass on

- experiences such as apprenticeships, travel, service, or career training

- pursuit of interests, hobbies, and passions

- state mandates for reporting and/or graduation requirements

Multimodal Experiences

Let's explore Ralph Tyler's next question a bit further: "What educational experiences can be provided that are likely to attain these purposes?" How does what we've learned so far about memory, concentration, motivation, and growth affect selecting educational experiences and assessing progress? Based on what we have learned so far, I would like to offer you some advice about selecting educational experiences. You may have noticed that several of the tools and techniques from the last chapter appeared on lists for more than one modality. Activities that appeal to multiple styles or all styles are called multimodal activities. They are desirable for two reasons.

First, multimodal activities allow teachers to cast a wider net in group activities. Making a folderbook or lapbook might appeal to visual learners because of the opportunity to draw, color, label, or describe items in the book; while kinesthetic learners get to engage their hands and enjoy cutting, gluing, taping, folding, and coloring. Same activity, different reasons for engagement. And their resulting products might look very different.

Second, multimodal experiences tend to form stronger memories than monomodal activities. As we engage more of our senses in a project, less irrelevant information makes it past the attention filter and into working memory. That means that our working memory has a higher effective load and a lower ineffective load. As we process information from multiple angles and with multiple senses, it stands a greater chance of being well encoded into long-term memory.

Therefore, look for curricula that include assignments and projects that appeal to a variety of learning preferences. Certainly, there is a place for curricula that are designed to focus on a specific modality. Some people do need, say, a kinesthetic approach to mathematics or a highly visual foreign language program. But as a general rule, I prefer multimodal instructional design. We have already talked about when to match or map and when to flex. The best curricula include more activities than any one family or classroom can possibly complete, with the assumption that teachers will choose only those activities that will best further their teaching goals. This is especially important when teaching more than one student at a time. In a homeschool setting, parents may even use the same curriculum for multiple ages simultaneously. You can select activities that will best fit your whole family's needs.

> *Multimodal experiences tend to form stronger memories than monomodal activities. As we engage more of our senses in a project, less irrelevant information makes it past the attention filter and into working memory.*

As you search for curriculum, remember that designing the experience is ultimately your responsibility. Use of a textbook or a video set is one experience among the many that you'll be curating. The text or video may appeal to the visual modality, and you then have the opportunity over the year to supplement it with other experiences that map or flex to your students' other modalities as you see fit. You likely won't have time to make every lesson multimodal, so think about appealing to multiple modalities over the course of the year rather than the course of the day. The book or lecture is one experience, but it doesn't need to be the only one.

A variety of educational experiences will meet more needs, form stronger neural connections, and build deeper and longer lasting memories than a single-modality approach. That variety may include offering different

VAK-based options for activities after a lesson, but why stop there? Consider field trips, internships and apprenticeships, work experience, project-based and problem-based learning, interviews with experts or eyewitnesses, or any number of other less-conventional experiences. The wider the variety, the better. There are always constraints, but a little creativity can go a long way toward overcoming them.

> *Variety of experience is useful only as far as it supports educational goals. Each activity should advance the purpose and weave another thread in the tapestry of learning.*

Keep in mind, though, that variety of experience is useful only as far as it supports educational goals. Each activity should advance the purpose and weave another thread in the tapestry of learning. A fun activity that has little bearing on the subject matter is best jotted down and saved for a more suitable future lesson. Don't lose sight of the big picture: select only those activities that actually advance your goals. You have only so much time and energy, so spend it wisely.

ASSESSMENT

We've discussed two of Ralph Tyler's questions. The third one is "How can these educational experiences be effectively organized?" If you're purchasing a curriculum set rather than designing your own from scratch, then this work is probably done for you. If not, you'll need to become enough of an expert on the subject matter to determine this for yourself. Since this book is not about curriculum design, we won't explore that here.

Finally, Tyler asks "How can we determine whether these purposes are being attained?" Assessments, both formal and informal, play an important role in any curriculum design. Unfortunately, there are two significant problems that undermine useful assessment in a homeschooling situation: credits and tests.

The Problem of Credits

The standard measurement of academic achievement for high school and beyond is the Carnegie Unit. Developed in the early 1900s by the Carnegie Foundation, a Carnegie Unit is a measure of student's exposure to material, and it represents 120 hours of classroom instruction in high school. Credits were originally designed to represent students' readiness for college in a uniform manner. College credit hours (also developed by the Carnegie Foundation) similarly measure instructional time, but they typically represent only about 15 hours. Graduating from high school might require 22 credits, but a four-year bachelor's degree might entail 120 credit hours.

Unfortunately, credits have taken on the task of measuring academic achievement as well. The problems with credits as a measure of achievement are clear. A student may spend copious amounts of time in a class without mastering the material. Another student may master the material quickly, well before the 120-hour mark. Despite their disparate achievement, both students can receive the same number of credits. Thus, credits and credit hours can mask the quality of students' learning by focusing on the quantity of instruction rather than the students' performance. The fact that "Cs get degrees" has become the unofficial motto of underperforming students across America. While grades and credits are distinct concepts, employers are typically more interested in whether or not a person has a diploma or a degree than in that person's GPA (a more revealing measurement).

Some homeschooling parents, aware that their states define credits purely in terms of hours of teacher contact, go to great lengths to ensure that their students receive suitable amounts of exposure. They log every hour of lecture, every book read and documentary watched, time spent in field trips, etc. We can expose students to new material for scores of hours, but without assessment, we have no way of telling if they have actually learned. While high levels of information exposure are certainly good and may satisfy state requirements, they don't necessarily mean that learning has occurred. Without a matching plan for student output (such as projects, feedback, reflection, and assessments), there's no real way to tell. And this hours-based approach to awarding credits doesn't offer any incentive for meaningful assessment. If a student's record can show that he or she has put in the hours, that's considered good enough.

This hours-based approach also hampers the ability of students to work at their own pace, which is one of the great benefits of homeschooling. A course that might take one student 120 hours or more to complete might be accomplished in half the time by another student. But the second student may be forced to plod along more slowly simply because it's not a full credit without all the hours.

However, these problems need not burden us. Some states allow students to earn credit by demonstrating mastery of course competencies. The details of that process will vary by state, and homeschoolers will need to determine how that might be accomplished on a case-by-case basis. Further, there are excellent, helpful ways to assess mastery that don't involve logging hours.

The Problem of Testing

Mastery of information, rather than quantity of exposure, should be at the heart of our instruction and assessment. Sadly, the primary value of testing is determining how well a student can take tests. Many tests, while thorough in the amount of content they cover, have significant downsides. They provide false negatives and false positives; that is, they penalize students who are poor test takers but actually do know the material, and they also allow students who are proficient test takers but have a weak grasp of the material to pass with high marks.

Testing problems are exacerbated as more and more testing is graded by computers, which are great at marking simple true/false, multiple-choice, and matching questions but are not capable of assessing essays or even short-answer questions reliably. Ease of grading is prioritized over the actual usefulness of assessments. As learning has become standardized, so has assessment.

Fortunately, most homeschoolers have already rejected the idea that standardized education is superior to individualized education. If we apply that reasoning to our assessment practices, a whole new world opens up for us as teachers. In fact, I much prefer the term *assessment* over *test* because *assessment* speaks to the purpose of the activity, while *test* speaks only to the format.

> *We need to leave behind the idea that a test is a series of questions on paper. There are many ways to meaningfully determine if students have learned what we want them to learn.*

We need to leave behind the idea that a test is a series of questions on paper. There are many ways to meaningfully determine if students have learned what we want them to learn. Remember what we covered back in chapter 1 on memory about the difference between cued recall and free recall? Cued recall (which is often the core of testing) only serves to show that they remember the right answer to a particular question. Free recall, by contrast, provides a window into everything they've learned about a topic. In that light, alternative assessment strategies can be relied on to provide much more useful feedback than a timed final exam filled with true/false or multiple-choice questions. Consider the following alternatives, each of which can more than adequately replace final exams and other periodic quizzes:

- oral examinations
- capstone projects
- thesis or research papers
- portfolio presentations or gallery exhibitions
- performances, recitations, and dramatizations

It's worth noting that oral examinations used to be the common practice among institutes of higher learning. They were replaced in the twentieth century in the interest of providing a more standardized method of evaluating students' knowledge, preventing examiners' biases from being problematic. Minimizing bias is a valid concern and part of the challenge of homeschooling. However auditory students in particular would be much better assessed by listening to their knowledge rather than asking them to write it down.

Of course, the test provided with a textbook may be necessary sometimes, especially when we parents haven't mastered the subject being taught. In such cases, there's nothing wrong with using a form of assessment that is conveniently graded and doesn't require us to be experts. When possible, however, the final examination need not default to a mere test.

Whatever method of assessment you choose, make sure that it is subservient to your goal. The goal of the class is not to put on a dramatization or complete a project any more than it is to prepare students to pass an arbitrary test. This is another reason why clear goals in curricula are so important. Teachers need to know what exactly we are attempting to assess.

Evaluating Curricula

Backward design is the idea that curriculum developers should start by establishing students' learning goals. From there, they decide how best to assess those goals, and then they design instruction that will enable students to pass the assessments. If you're familiar with Stephen Covey's excellent *7 Habits of Highly Effective People*, you might recognize this as an extension of habit 2: "Begin with the end in mind" (2013, 102). It's simple advice, but it makes a world of difference.

As you're choosing textbooks and programs to use with your students, keep these questions in mind:

- Are the goals of this program clear? Do they fit with my philosophy of education and goals?

- Are there meaningful assessments? If not, could I come up with some myself?

- Does the instruction plan include activities for the modalities that are most important to my family?

- Does this program make use of important concepts of learning science, such as spaced review, free recall practice, and an awareness of the limitations of students' working memory?

Every program has strengths and weaknesses, but good curriculum will do as much of the work for you as possible. You may have to compensate for the weaknesses yourself—which is fine if you're willing and able. While much more could be said about curriculum and instructional design, if you keep these questions and principles in mind while planning your school year, you will be building on a solid foundation.

KEY POINTS

▷ Thinking through our philosophy of education and our educational goals is important to do before picking out textbooks.

▷ Curriculum that emphasizes multimodal experiences is preferable to monomodal curricula. Good curriculum does the hard, creative work for us.

▷ Mastery of material is far more important than approaches based on time or exposure.

▷ Assessment is not the same as testing. Effective assessments can take many forms and can be tailored to the student's learning style, the subject matter, and circumstances.

Conclusion
Tying It All
Together

Good News

We've discussed some of the most influential theories of learning styles, yet we've only scratched the surface. There is more to read and research than we could explore in a short survey such as this. Are your children left-brained, right-brained, or middle brained? Are they global or analytical? Are they concrete or abstract, sequential or random? Are they social or independent learners? How do their personalities and interests intersect with all of this?

If you're fired up and want to learn more, that's great! Browse through the reference list and find some further reading. But before you add another shelf of books to your personal library, test these ideas for yourself. Make notes on how they work, notice your kids' preferences and reactions, and spend time reflecting before you dig deeper. Reflection aids your ability to remember and apply—not just your students'.

Perhaps you're already overwhelmed. If that's the case, take a deep breath. You probably don't need to completely overhaul your educational plan based on anything in this book. It's OK if you've identified weak points in your teaching—we all have them. Reread the bullet-point chapter summaries. Ask yourself, "What's one simple thing I can do differently this week using this information?" That's a great start. Don't get locked into analysis paralysis. Remember: done is better than perfect.

It would be a mistake to look at learning styles as the educational holy grail and the key to solving all our teaching problems. The researchers who have tried to find that key have failed so far. But they've definitely uncovered some useful treasures along the way.

If we think of our teaching as a building, then knowing the ways in which we all learn, applying memory theory, and managing cognitive load form a good foundation. Understanding our intelligences, fostering a growth mindset, and establishing well-developed goals form a solid frame. Our personal preferences of environment and individual motivation techniques make up the paint color and decor. Make sure your foundation is solid and your framing is square before you worry too much about window dressing.

We could examine plenty of other theories, questions, models, and measurements. However, I've chosen the theories and ideas in this book because they're the ones that I have found have the most accessible and useful for our education practice and because they represent the most common questions I hear on the subject. My hope is that after finishing this short work, you'll have enough information to go on and you'll feel equipped to get started using the powers of memory, concentration, motivation, skill, and curriculum to benefit your homeschool.

Summary of Key Points

Memory

1. Our three memory banks are sensory memory, working memory, and long-term memory.

2. Information moves from working memory to long-term memory through a dialogue between new and prior knowledge.

3. The more sensory connections and prior knowledge connections we make, the easier it will be to recall new information in the future.

4. Cued recall = fill-in-the-blank. Free recall = essay question. Spaced, free-recall sessions with immediate feedback are one the most effective strategies for studying material.

Concentration

1. Working memory holds a very limited amount of information at a time. Don't overload it!

2. Ineffective load (wasted working memory) can be caused by internal or external factors. Deal with those as best you can before digging into new material.

3. Environmental preferences vary from person to person. To reduce distraction, make students feel comfortable while they learn whenever possible.

4. Multitasking slows us down and causes errors.

Motivation

1. Extrinsic motivation (carrots and sticks) works only for dull, repetitive tasks. Intrinsic motivation (mastery, autonomy, and purpose) is required for everything else.

2. Learning modalities are preferences, not prerequisites. They predict engagement, not achievement.

3. Visual, auditory, and kinesthetic learners are more likely to fully engage in different kinds of activities.

4. Mapping is best for areas in which students are already demotivated. Flexing is useful for building skills and challenging them in areas where they're already motivated or talented.

GROWTH

1. There is more than one way to be smart.

2. Understanding our multiple intelligences can help us appreciate and communicate with our students.

3. We can grow in all of our intelligences through diligent effort, study, and good teaching.

4. While we don't have to include every intelligence in every lesson, we should be aware of which intelligences we're developing and be intentional about doing so.

CURRICULUM

1. Thinking through our philosophy of education and our educational goals is important to do before picking out textbooks.

2. Curriculum that emphasizes multimodal experiences is preferable to monomodal curricula. Good curriculum does the hard, creative work for us.

3. Mastery of material is far more important than approaches based on time or exposure.

4. Assessment is not the same as testing. Effective assessments can take many forms and can be tailored to the student's learning style, the subject matter, and circumstances.

Akplotsyi, R. and L. Mahdjoubi. 2011. "Effects of Learning Styles on Engaging Children in School Projects." *ARCOM* (5th–7th September 2011): 331–339.
The paper that indicates VAK modalities produce greater quantities of engagement in modal-specific activities.

Armstrong, Thomas. 2014. *You're Smarter Than You Think: A Kid's Guide to Multiple Intelligences.* Golden Valley, MN: Free Spirit Publishing Inc. ISBN: 978-1-57542-431-6.
Great for students and teachers. Applies multiple intelligence theory to show how we can all grow in each area and recommends strategies for using certain abilities to complement or compensate for others.

Austen, Jane. (1813) 2001. *Pride and Prejudice.* Edited by Donald Gray. New York and London: W. W. Norton.

Carey, Benedict. 2014. *How We Learn.* New York: Random House. ISBN 978-0-8129-8429-3.
Provides helpful information on effective study skills.

Connell, Diane J. 2005. *Brain-Based Strategies to Reach Every Learner.* New York: Scholastic. ISBN 0-439-59020-5.
One of my favorites—a great follow-up to this book. Filled with useful assessments for a number of models as well as very practical application for each idea.

Covey, Stephen R. 2013. *The 7 Habits of Highly Effective People: Powerful Lessons in Personal Change.* New York: Simon & Schuster. ISBN 978-1-4767-4005-8.
Covey's classic work has great value in understanding goal-setting (habit 2) and developing the growth mindset (habits 1 and 7).

Dweck, Carol. 2014. *The Power of Believing That You Can Improve.* TED. Retrieved from https://www.ted.com/talks/carol_dweck_the_power_of_believing_that_you_can_improve.
A great introduction to the growth mindset, which is explored further in Dweck's book.

———. 2016. *Mindset: The New Psychology of Success*. New York: Ballantine Books. ISBN 978-0-345-47232-8.
A deeper dive into mindsets, including their influence in sports, business, and relationships as well as how mindsets change.

Gardner, Howard. 2011. *Frames of Mind: The Theory of Multiple Intelligences*. New York: Basic Books. ISBN 978-0-465-02433-9.
Lengthy and more technical than most of the books on this list but filled with insight if you want to dig deep into MI theory.

Gershon, Mike. 2015. *How to Use Bloom's Taxonomy in the Classroom*. www.MikeGershon.com. Self-published in the UK. ISBN 978-1-51743201-0.
Part of a series of short, practical books for teachers. Easy read with plenty of application.

Kane, Pearl R. and Kevin Mattingly. 2018. *The Science of Learning: What Every Teacher Should Know*. New York: Teachers College, Columbia University. Retrieved from: https://courses.edx.org/courses/course-v1:TeachersCollegeX+EDSCI1x+1T2018/course/.
I highly recommend this excellent free course on cognitive science in the classroom. In particular, the first unit deals helpfully with memory theory and cognitive load.

King, Martin Luther, Jr. 1947. "The Purpose of Education." *The Maroon Tiger* (January-February 1947): 10. Accessed September 24, 2018. https://kinginstitute.stanford.edu/king-papers/documents/purpose-education.

Koch, Kathy. 2016. *8 Great Smarts*. Chicago: Moody Publishers. ISBN 978-0-8024-1359-8.
Helps parents understand and appreciate their kids' abilities from the standpoint of multiple intelligence theory.

Pashler, H., M. McDaniel, D. Rohrer, and R. Bjork. 2008. "Learning Styles: Concepts and Evidence." *Psychological Science in the Public Interest* (Wiley-Blackwell), 9 (3): 105–119.
Establishes criteria for testing the mapping hypothesis and analyzes some of the studies that have been performed.

Pink, Daniel H. 2009. *Drive: The Surprising Truth About What Motivates Us.* New York: Riverhead Books. ISBN 978-1-59448-884-9. *While not specifically about education, many of the principles are widely applicable to teaching and parenting as well as the workplace.*

Plutarch. 1992. "On Listening." In *Essays,* 27–50. London and New York: Penguin Books. ISBN 978-0140445640.

Salomon, G. 1984. "Television Is 'Easy' and Print Is 'Tough': The Differential Investment of Mental Effort in Learning as a Function of Perceptions and Attributions." *Journal of Educational Psychology* 76 (4): 647–658. *Discusses why students may not learn as much if the material is too easy.*

Tobias, Cynthia U. 1994. *The Way They Learn.* Colorado Springs, CO: Focus on the Family. ISBN 1-56179-253-5. *A bit outdated but discusses some of the models we didn't cover here, including Gregorc's perception and ordering model and global/ analytic variables.*

Tyler, Ralph W. 1949. *Basic Principles of Curriculum and Instruction.* Chicago: The University of Chicago Press. ISBN 978-0-226-08650-7. *A classic text on curriculum development and planning.*

U. S. Department of Education. 2018. "Overview and Mission Statement." Accessed September 21. https://www2.ed.gov/about/landing.jhtml.

Willingham, Daniel T. 2009. *Why Don't Students Like School?* San Francisco: Jossey-Bass. ISBN 978-0-470-59196-3. *A wonderful Q&A on cognitive science and teaching. Part science journalism, part educational myth-busting.*

Willis, Mariaemma and Victoria K. Hodson. 1999. *Discover Your Child's Learning Style.* New York: Three Rivers Press. ISBN 0-7615-2013-9 *Best feature is the holistic "Learning Style Profile Assessments" and accompanying documentation. Also explores some disposition models not covered here.*

Wilkinson, Bruce. 1992. *The Seven Laws of the Learner.* Sisters, OR: Multnomah Publishers. ISBN 1-59052-452-7. *By far the most powerful and helpful book on teaching I've ever read.*

By Emily Haller, RD

- Plain Greek yogurt topped with blueberries
  - ▷ Blueberries are packed with antioxidants that support healthy brain cells.

- Carrots and cucumbers with hummus
  - ▷ Combination of protein and fiber stabilizes blood sugar to keep you alert.

- Apples with peanut butter
  - ▷ Mix of healthy fat and protein fills you up and keeps you full.

- Fruit smoothie with spinach
  - ▷ Greens provide vitamins associated with alertness and memory.

- Trail mix with dark chocolate, nuts, raisins, and coconut chips
  - ▷ Magnesium in dark chocolate helps increase blood flow to the brain.

- Buttered popcorn (Avoid the microwave bag!)
  - ▷ Fiber from this whole-grain, low-cal snack plus healthy fat can curb your appetite.

- Hard-boiled egg topped with avocado slice
  - ▷ Eggs are a good source of choline, which supports memory and cognition.

- Banana chia pudding
  - ▷ Omega-3 fatty acids from chia seeds in this naturally sweetened snack help improve attention.

- Frozen grapes
  - ▷ This naturally sweetened treat hydrates and refreshes.

- String cheese
  - ▷ This is a portion-controlled source of calcium.

TYLER HOGAN

Tyler Hogan is the president of Bright Ideas Press. He and his wife, Helen, are both homeschool graduates and now homeschool their five adorable children. Tyler is the author of *North Star Geography* and *Demystifying Learning Styles*, head cartographer of WonderMaps, and game designer of Civitas.

When not at home, he speaks and teaches about home-schooling, geography, the arts, worldview, entrepreneurship, and other topics. He is an elder at Grace Church, where he also serves as Christian Education Coordinator. In his spare time, he loves reading good books, playing games with friends, drinking good tea, and enjoying the adventure of lifelong learning. He has a BA in theatre ministries from Belhaven University.

CPSIA information can be obtained
at www.ICGtesting.com
Printed in the USA
BVHW010919170422
634374BV00002B/20